Out of UNIFORM

A Career Transition Guide for Ex-Military Personnel

Out of UNIFORM

A Career Transition Guide for Ex-Military Personnel

Foreword by Joyce Lain Kennedy

Harry N. Drier

Printed on recyclable paper

VGM Career Horizons
a division of *NTC Publishing Group*
Lincolnwood, Illinois USA

Library of Congress Cataloging-in-Publication Data

Drier, Harry N.
    Out of uniform : a career transition guide for ex-military
personnel / Harry N. Drier, Jr.
        p.   cm.
    Includes bibliographical references.
    ISBN 0-8442-4384-1
    1. Career changes—United States.   2. Retired military personnel—
Employment—United States.   3. Veterans—Employment—United States.
4. Job hunting—United States.   I. Title.
HF5384.D75   1995
650.14'024355—dc20   94-28734
                                                                        CIP

Published by VGM Career Horizons, a division of NTC Publishing Group
4255 West Touhy Avenue
Lincolnwood (Chicago), Illinois 60646-1975, U.S.A.
© 1995 by NTC Publishing Group. All rights reserved.
No part of this book may be reproduced, stored in a retrieval
system, or transmitted in any form or by any means,
electronic, mechanical, photocopying, recording or otherwise,
without the prior permission of NTC Publishing Group.
Manufactured in the United States of America.

4 5 6 7 8 9 0 ML 9 8 7 6 5 4 3 2 1

Contents

Acknowledgments

This book was developed by a team of experts, selected because of their previous military service and current involvement in a range of outplacement and employee transition efforts.

Mr. Henry Button, President, College Decision Systems, is a disabled military veteran and served in the Vietnam campaign. Mr. Button contributed information on college selection, financial aid, and military benefits.

Mr. Gary Blair, President, Blair Leadership Enterprises, writes extensively on personal goal development for individuals in transition. He contributed a wealth of material dealing with goal setting, career planning, and case studies that will be useful to military personnel and family members in transition.

Special thanks are extended to Dr. Janet Wall, Manpower Data Systems, for her guidance throughout the preparation of the manuscript. Her insights into the military structure and transition process were key to the final format and chapter focus. Additionally, the book would not have been completed without the day-to-day management, advice, and leadership of my editor, Sarah Kennedy. Her keen insight, professional prodding of the author to meet deadlines, and creative recommendations for improving the book were invaluable. Likewise, Amy Yu, the designer, brought life into the text with her creative design recommendations. Together they have made this book most reader friendly and accurate.

Last, appreciation is given to Ms. Mary LaBelle, Mrs. Beverly Haynes, and Ms. Carlene Hamilton for their manuscript preparation assistance. Together they turned rough thoughts into helpful ideas.

Harry Drier has himself served in the U.S. Army, and has published extensively for various military branches. As the Chairperson for the National Career Development Association's Military Special Interest Group he has met and worked with experts on military career issues including those above and others too numerous to mention. He appreciates the impact all of those peers have had on his knowledge of the field and the development of this book.

Foreword

To Each Man and Woman Who Is—or Is About To Be—"Out of Uniform"

★★

You are beginning a daring and epic journey to the rest of your life. The decisions you make at this fork in the road—today, tomorrow, next week, next month—can cast a future that is either bright or grim.

Until now you've anticipated most days before they began. You've known what would be expected of you, and how you were likely to spend your minutes and hours. Your money was certain, your vacations were set, and your boss wore stripes.

Now your life is different. The outline of tomorrow is a little murky, even scary, as you realize that the traditional values of company loyalty and job security are nearly dead in the 1990s.

As you leave service life, you probably have little certainty about what lies ahead—exactly how you'll spend your time, how much money you'll have, what you'll be expected to achieve. And your boss will be wearing civvies.

This is the time—right now!—to put your best effort into the process of passage from military to civilian status. When you consider that half a billion new people will enter the global workforce this decade and that 90 percent of them will be in countries such as Mexico and China that pay low wages, you'll agree that if you don't want to work cheaper, you'd better work smarter to maintain the comfort of living in a first-world nation.

It's an undisputed fact: Manual labor in first-world countries cannot compete with manual labor in underdeveloped countries, where wages are but a fraction of ours.

Harry Drier is knowledgeable about these economics, as well as other trends of the workplace. Harry knows that, much as the railroads set the pace for the 19th century, and as natural resources and manufacturing did for most of the 20th, software and communications industries are the front runners for the 21st century.

This is why it is so urgent for you to consider becoming what economists call knowledge labor, not manual labor.

Some of you will earn your living in pure knowledge labor jobs. You'll work almost exclusively with your heads as network engineers and accountants, marketing directors and financial specialists. Indeed, you may have gotten a head start with your military training. But the world is moving so fast that even the trees appear to be a blurred streak of shades of green.

That's why you must strive to add to your skills, to keep them up to date and to take advantage of all professional development opportunities. Otherwise you can quickly become outdated.

The need to become a member of the knowledge labor force does not mean you can't work with your hands. The nation will always need plumbers and landscapers, repairers and store managers. In this case, becoming a knowledge labor person means you must learn to work with your head—as well as with your hands.

Options on the best ways to find your place in the world of knowledge labor are the very things Harry shares with you in this book.

No mere ivory-tower theorist, Harry Drier was a seasoned veteran of the workplace trenches before his assignments at Ohio State University, where he became a prominent and highly regarded member of the national counseling community. Now president of Career, Education & Training Associates, Inc. in Columbus, Ohio, Harry understands that you are losing not only a job, but a way of life. He knows that you don't want to be immobilized in a holding action any longer than necessary. He knows that you don't want a 500-page tome with nonstop reading that takes eons to tell you what you should do next.

That's why Harry Drier has written a reliable, solid, down-to-earth guide with a winning philosophy:

Reveal what the career hunter must know now. And cut to the chase.

So, let's go! Turn the page and travel with Harry on your daring and epic journey to the rest of your sunny life.

Joyce Lain Kennedy
Syndicated Careers Columnist

Introduction

It's time to leave the Armed Forces. You're now attempting re-entry into a traditional situation, and that transition is difficult. For many adults, changing jobs, employers, or locations brings anxiety, fear, frustration, and unrest. Being dislocated from a career and employer that you've grown to know, depend on, and trust can be a psychologically shocking experience. You may see your economic stability, social life, and sense of belonging as "at risk." Experienced veterans like you have had a job niche that provided pride, satisfaction, and a sense of belonging. Working and living outside the traditional labor market—and, at times, the traditional social environment—creates a sense of anxiety about the knowledge of civilian networks, resources, and services needed for re-entry into the environment. This is especially true for veterans with family members who also face major transitions and changes in their lives.

This book offers suggestions on how this major career change can be a positive adventure if it is well thought out. As a veteran, you often cannot see the sizable advantages of the training, work experience, credentials, and employment skills you gained while working for the nation's largest employer. Employers realize the state-of-the-art training and retraining that is provided and expected of the U.S. Armed Forces. They envy the military approach and expectations regarding employee work behavior and productivity. The standards held for a military worker's professional and social life serve as models for major employers.

Your valued career experience in the military can put you at the front of the line for career opportunities. Industry will see the benefit of experience, especially in key supervisory and leadership positions. Businesses need mature

1

managers who can begin producing profit immediately. Government agencies need dependable and tested managers. The U.S. economy is wide open for entrepreneurs, and Third World countries' economic growth is dependent on skilled and experienced consultants. The choice is yours. It's a buyer's market today, and you have a product that is in high demand.

Preparing for the Adventure
★★

This book is organized around the many issues that you will face or are currently facing as you make your transition. The following are a series of "get-ready" suggestions to help you take full advantage of the opportunities before you.

Attitude

Yes, there are excellent opportunities available to you as a veteran. You need to view being "out of uniform" as a positive step to your new career. If you view this transition as an opportunity, it will unfold. If you view it as intimidating, worrisome, or stressful, opportunities may not become evident and thus be lost. As a veteran, you've been trained to handle high-stress situations; this is the time to use these skills.

★★★★★

"Those who have goals reach them; those without goals, don't."

★★★★★

Taking Advantage of the System

If you are still in the military, be sure to take advantage of the services available, including the following:

★ Visit your educational center and access all their information.

★ Seek out your retirement counselor.

★ Attend all the seminars and workshops available under your Transition Assistance Program (TAP).

★ Obtain full documentation of all educational benefits available to you and family members.

★ Make appointments for all possible dental, vision, and health services before separation. This will give you more time to focus on other issues when you arrive home, plus save a lot of money.

★ Check out all options for health, life, and auto insurance needs and opportunities. What do you maintain? What new policies do you need?

★ Have someone explain all the advantages of obtaining Veterans' Administration loans, if you're interested in buying a home, business, and so on.

★ Begin checking out the rent/lease/home-purchase options in the city you're moving to. There are multi-state, national, and international real estate firms that can begin the search for you if you have some idea of what your needs are and what your resources can handle.

★ What about your transportation needs? What is the most efficient and cost-effective way to get home? Will you need a car/transportation once you reach your new home? If so, you'll need a reliable dealer to assist you in selecting transportation that's within your budget.

★ Have you considered making transition to the Reserves or National Guard? If so, what can you do before leaving your base to make all the needed arrangements?

★ Clothing, both type and quantity, may be a concern when you return to civilian life. Think through your projected needs and take advantage of your base-available options. They might save you some real money.

★ You'll need to do a language check. How does your "militarese" need to be tempered for the nonveteran employer or neighbor. You've got many unique abbreviations, slang terms, and so forth that you will not be able to use in your new setting.

★ One way of getting comfortable in a new setting is to become involved in the community. Check out the many options available in your community (American Legion, Parent-Teacher Association, Boy or Girl Scouts, Lions Club, and many more). Getting everyone in the family involved in a sport of choice is a quick way to make friends in your new home.

★ Education for your family could be an issue. Obtain information about public and private school options before moving. Your home selection could depend on being in a city that has the special educational programs you need.

★ Selecting a health team or plan in advance could save you difficulty once you arrive. Contact a friend or a community agency for information about the physicians, dentists, and other health professionals you'll need as soon as you arrive home. This process takes time, so start early.

★ Subscribe to the newspaper that serves the city you're moving to. You can examine information about jobs, housing, community events, and local cost of living for at least one month before you arrive.

Using this Book

There are simple ways of preparing for all aspects of your transition, and this book could help. It is intended to be a desk reference, so the material is organized in three categories. The first 14 chapters cover targeted issues and have a host of hints on how to cope with each important aspect of your transition. They are followed by a "methods section" of short, hard-hitting checklists, examples, and formats for seven specific tasks you will need to perform. The appendixes are more informational, and you may want to refer to them from time to time for more information on a specific topic, like foreign opportunities.

Remember, this transition may be only a separation from the military, not a full termination. There are many ways of keeping in touch with your friends and services from the Armed Forces. There are also a number of ways you can serve in a more inactive way in the military. We will cover these ideas in later chapters as well.

★★★★★

"Plan to succeed and if you do, indeed you'll win."

★★★★★

The Psychology of Transition

This chapter is about recognizing what is going to happen, identifying what you want to change, knowing what is beyond your control, and, above all, realizing that some of your most maddening concerns are normal. The secret, of course, is knowing about everything in advance.

This is the end of one way of life and the beginning of another. It marks the completion of one career and the first day of a new one. It represents the greatest lifestyle change most of you will ever experience. It means putting down roots after decades of moving every two or three years. It may signify the end of family separations. Old stresses are replaced by new ones. Everything changes.

Once you know when you will leave active duty, you also know how much time you have to prepare. Prepare for what, leaving active duty? The service takes care of that. You're processed out with the same efficiency as when you joined. How about preparing for the new job? Well, that's certainly necessary. But, what *is* the new job? If you can't answer that, how can you prepare for it?

All of these questions are part of a much larger one that only you can answer, and answer as soon as possible: "What am I going to be?" Those who know what they're going to be and when they're going to make it happen have the transition battle half won. Imagine that you have both of those answers. Any new problems relating to resumés, salary, location, housing, or other requirements are easily addressed because you can be specific. You have narrowed the field, and you can concentrate on the options that fit your choice.

Once you decide on a realistic job goal, you have some idea about where the jobs are, the salary range within which you should begin, and what housing you should be able to afford; you can also establish some contacts, scout out an area with military facilities, and, above all, give your transition preparation a direction.

Knowing when you will step out of uniform gives you another edge. Without a specific date, your preparations are only contingency planning; a certain goal gives your transition some form of organization.

Direction and organization: With them, you can begin civilian life with both feet on the ground; without them, you may drift until necessity decides your future for you. It's hard to find anyone beginning a transition who will admit that he or she is concerned about a job or money. The truth is, just about everyone worries about these things. Combined with questions about medical care, benefits, financial planning, inflation, housing, and other issues, they can result in a tremendous mental burden.

Facing Reality

★★★

You are going to be, or are now, a civilian. It doesn't happen only to the other person. During active duty, we gear our lives to mission accomplishment. If we think about our own transition, it's usually in a "what I'm going to do when I get out of this chicken outfit" way, in the middle of another inspection preparation, field exercise, or Sunday alert. Serious consideration and planning come later, when transition time is just around the corner.

Leaving the service is a major milestone. If you plan reasonably well, it needn't be a traumatic one. Begin planning within yourself. Recognize that you're going to have plenty of questions swimming around in your head, that the questions are normal, and that you won't have answers to them all right now. Thousands of people face the same situation each year, and they have the same questions, plus some of their own. When doubts surface (and they will), it's important to know that you're in a normal situation, not one you've caused by some oversight or neglect. Once you're mentally prepared, you'll find it much easier to deal with the other aspects of transition, such as your spouse's situation, the house, the car, finances, insurance, the job market, and the children's education.

You're not old and you're not giving up. As a matter of fact, you're in an enviable position. Get into the proper frame of mind and enjoy it fully. When these doubts we talked about start gnawing at you, put them into perspective.

If you're going to have any control over this transition, you've got to identify exactly what's happening. If you know what's coming, there's no reason to be unprepared. A lot happens during a major career change, especially when it's from the military to civilian life. You must (a) anticipate what's coming, (b) recognize it as normal, and (c) break the transition process into manageable pieces so that you can cope with each challenge as it surfaces.

Moving On
★★

Your last day arrives. It can be marked by anything from just leaving work early to a simple ceremony to a parade. It's amazing how many people just want to ease out. After all's said and done, the ultimate measure of "tough" might be that last national anthem in uniform. As an outgoing soldier once said, "Anyone who can handle that with dry eyes should be shot for treason." But no matter how you go out, at the end of the day, it's over.

The Adjustment Phase

On the first day after retirement from the service, even if you've done everything right, you'll start one of the major adjustments of your life. The "adjustment phase" begins full force. No basic training, no drill sergeant, and no transition period. One day you're in, the next day, you're out—period.

The job transition, if all goes well, can smooth a lot of rough spots at home. But the entire family must make adjustments, and they have little to do with the job. They start when you, as a family, realize you have some role adjustments to cope with.

In the service, everything is based on rank and precedence. Income, although related to rank, is secondary, but housing, job, family status, and just about everything else is tied to your position in the military society. And you know just where to go to accomplish just about anything. If there are problems, you know how to solve them and who is in charge. In civilian life, military rank and status don't matter anymore. There seems to be a structure, but it's almost impossible to figure out. Status still depends on how you fit into society, but you have to know the rules. Ever try drawing an organizational chart of a civilian community?

You start feeling the difference after a month as a civilian. Until now, it's been like a month's leave, and you've enjoyed it. But the years of conditioning to the military system seem to tell you, "Orders are on the way, it's time to move on." There aren't any more orders. No one's telling you what to do. There's no "outfit," no chain of command, and no one waiting with open arms for you to save the organization. As a matter of fact, a month after you're gone, the service has filled the hole, and your old comrades are getting on with the show. Your name may be mentioned now and then.

The familiar signs and symbols are gone. It's easy to measure a person's success in the service. Out here, any visible signs aren't so easy to read. Your ego takes another blow as you realize that civilians don't really care about your former status. Out here, you'll be measured by a different yardstick: So far as they're concerned, you're the "new guy." It's tough on your confidence, this business of adapting to civilian life. Sure, you've lived "on the economy" before, maybe even owned a house or two, but your life still centered on the military world. About now, you start realizing the vast differences between these two ways of life.

The Elements of Stress

Virtually everyone experiences some stress during times of transition. Some people accept job change in a matter-of-fact manner and adjust easily to change and new situations. Others have trouble coping and essentially become ineffective job candidates. Few of us can make a job change without experiencing some stress. The very necessity of reporting for a job interview is enough to cause some people to enter an excited, and sometimes fearful, state.

Whether a job search or change of job involves stress depends a lot on the individual. The person's qualifications, financial condition, self-confidence, and ability to adjust to unfamiliar situations are all potential contributors to stress.

Good planning can help reduce job-search stress, but will not completely eliminate it. An awareness of the types of stresses you will face can help you cope. In some cases, the only way to diagnose the stress is through identification of the symptoms that accompany it. The following subsections identify some of the most common forms of stresses experienced during a job search.

Emotional Stress

Among the various emotional crises one can experience during a lifetime, loss of a job rates very high in stress quotient, along with the death of a family member, divorce, and bankruptcy. The same types of spillover consequences that accompany other high-stress situations follow the loss of a job. The loss can be imposed externally, as in a firing, or it may be a voluntary separation. Nevertheless, stress is still present. The status quo has been shattered. Even with routine changes, a period of evaluation and reflection sets in, and you have stress.

The emotional impact of a loss or change of job is tremendous. Until you've experienced unemployment, you cannot truly appreciate its attendant stresses. Don't overestimate your ability to cope with them. Recognize their ability to affect you and do your best to understand and deal with them so they can't overwhelm you.

Financial Stress

There are very few people who have not experienced some form of financial stress. When it results in fear of not being able to provide for the basics of living, such as food, clothing, and shelter, financial stress becomes a very serious matter. People lose their "normal" way of thinking and acting and go into a survival mode, which can work wonders for motivation, but the penalties paid in stress are high.

Other types of stresses may be somewhat less debilitating, but will still present significant challenges, thus every attempt should be made to reduce financial stress. The three key factors in your ability to reduce financial stress require planning. These key factors are as follows:

★ Sufficient funds to guarantee survival for a reasonable period of time

★ A budget plan that limits expenditures to necessities

★ A plan to eliminate or reduce the period of unemployment

Assuming that you're prudent enough to make these efforts, let's look at some of the financial stresses they can help relieve.

There is an immediate necessity to reevaluate your lifestyle. You must eliminate the fat in your budget for disposable income purchases. Luxuries, such as eating out and planned vacations are obvious targets for elimination. The less resources you have for such expenditures, the sooner you should eliminate them. If you and your family can accept these cuts gracefully for the length of time necessary, the stress will be reduced. Typically, it takes the impact of unpaid bills and crisis money management before people grudgingly accept cuts. By then, however, fear, frustration, anger, and feelings of inadequacy have set in, and the symptoms of financial stress take their toll.

The fear of losing one's possessions because of an inability to meet monthly payments becomes extremely serious when the roof over your head is involved. The injured pride factor in losing a home is bad enough, but where you will live next becomes a real problem.

The immediate necessity of altering lifestyles has an effect on each member of the family. Old habits die hard. If youngsters are affected, their lack of realization that the source of funds has dried up only adds fuel to the fire. Family arguments between spouses most often involve money, sex, or lack of appreciation for the other person. These powerful influences can shatter a marriage quickly.

Financial stress comes in many forms. The frustration of being unable to remove the cause of the stress, namely, lack of money, only brings more frustration.

Ego Stress

Each of us has a perception of our own relationship or relative position vis-à-vis the demands of our social and physical environment. When something unfavorably affects that perception, there is stress.

In the development of modern society, the trappings of ego building give us standards against which to compare our own performance. Basic survival has few elements of ego. The mind and body are too involved in mere living to assimilate a complex system of ego. Earning power, title, education level, possessions, and authority over others are at the top of the list of ego builders that we nurture and protect. Social relationships and acceptance by others are other important ego builders, as well.

So many ego factors are affected by one's job that the loss of it can become a traumatic experience. Being in a job that gives little ego satisfaction is somewhat better than no job at all. It provides for basic survival and gives foundation for ego building. When a person is unemployed, many of the reinforcements of ego building are removed, and he or she must operate on residual trappings. In some cases, those trappings are considerable and help sustain the person until reinforcement arrives.

A healthy, properly directed ego is good and necessary for a person's well-being in modern society. Ego building goes hand-in-hand with confidence building. Shatter one, and the other suffers.

Lack of Confidence

The confidence we have in our own knowledge and abilities is paramount to job success. It permits us to take on tasks we would otherwise avoid as being beyond our capabilities.

The longer you are unemployed, the less confident you are in your own abilities. In this situation, your mind is playing a dirty trick on you. Your abilities are no less than they were when you were employed (unless they involve a complex skill that requires frequent exercises). It's just that the symptoms of stress overpower your confidence in your abilities.

Lack of confidence is sometimes brought about by lack of demand for your knowledge and skills. Once the demand is discovered, a miraculous transformation takes place in your confidence level.

If, as a job-seeker, you must apply your knowledge and skills to unrelated requirements, or if your skills are inadequate to the task, your confidence in those skills is reduced. The stress of inadequacy is heaped on lack of confidence, and the problem is compounded.

If you lack confidence in your own abilities, you will not excite the prospective employer. He or she is looking for an employee who has the confidence to make a positive contribution to the company through competent performance. If you come across as lacking that confidence, your chances of being hired are slim indeed.

Once your confidence in your abilities drops, strange psychological, and even physiological, symptoms occur. Psychologically, you may become depressed and evasive or take the opposite tack and become arrogant and defensive. In either case, your job-search effectiveness is reduced. You may be reduced to a shy, stammering individual who won't look the interviewer in the eye and gazes at the floor or a remote object. At this stage, you are a candidate for psychological counseling. Your job search may have to be deferred to allow you time to regain your confidence.

Loss of Identity

For military people making the transition to civilian life after years of service, there is the potential for stress from a loss of identity. The structured environment of military service gives them a firm identity within the framework of rank, organization, and service. They wear the same uniform day in and day out, year after year. They are accorded the courtesies and perquisites associated with their rank and job assignment. They work, communicate, and socialize with people who understand their language and respect their position. Suddenly, all this changes.

Some people have trouble letting go of those things they understand and relate to. Civilians may neither recognize nor particularly respect their past accomplishments. Daily reinforcement of their identity ceases, and they become confused, frightened, and disoriented. They are under stress, and they don't quite know how to cope with it.

If you are having trouble adjusting, probably the best thing to do is seek counseling. The next best course of action is to take some time off and not plunge directly into a new job; give yourself time to make the transition and adjust to civilian life at a slower pace. You don't give up any of your values, but you can find new ways of expressing them in a different environment. The hardest part may be to avoid living in the past. You must find new challenges and a new identity. Sometimes that takes time, and patience is probably not your strongest attribute.

If you are ambitious, the problem will probably resolve itself quicker than if the drive for achievement is missing. In any case, you should begin the search for a new identity that doesn't need to satisfy anyone but yourself. This will probably be your biggest stumbling block. You can become so accustomed to a pleasing system with well-defined norms that when that system is removed, you can lose the ability to substitute anything for it. In this case, ask yourself, "What do I have to offer?" and "Who could use these attributes?" Ultimately, you must look inside yourself for the answers. You should realize that you do have a lot to offer, you just haven't taken the time to identify those things in terms of a market. Good research can identify potential markets and help you find a new identity. You will still have to adjust to that new identity, but the fact that you are making an effort to find it will be half the battle. Let go of the past. Push on to the new challenges. You can handle it.

Handling the Challenge
★★★

Slipping through a career without a hitch is nearly unheard of. No matter how much you plan and organize, there will be a surprise or two. Remember all those trips you took over the years while you were in the service. Each member of the family had individual responsibilities, and one of yours was loading the car. The first few times you had everything loaded just right, and then someone came along with another suitcase or a weird-shaped item (a hobby horse or a beach chair). You unloaded and reorganized everything and found to your amazement that it all fit. After a couple of those experiences, you beat the system by leaving room for a large suitcase. The space was always filled at the last minute with a ''surprise'' item. You never knew what it would be, but you were ready for the unknown.

What strategy should you adopt to be ready for transition? First, determine your answer to the question, ''What am I going to be?'' Once you can answer that, you have direction. Your thinking and efforts will be directed toward a specific goal, and every action you take will get you a little closer to it. Some other practical steps to take in preparation are given in the following section.

A Grocery List of Things to Do Today

1. Above all, learn about the career transition phenomenon. Think about it and research it. Pick up a book on the subject now and then; read it; note any items you need to take care of. Keep educating yourself.

2. The most important move you can make is to start early. Develop some long-term goals beyond a military rank or position and start planning to achieve those goals. The earlier you start, the easier your transition will be. It's a lot easier to make a simple change than to start from zero in the middle of a career change. Do it now.

3. Develop some roles outside the military community. It's unbelievable how few people do this. When the cord is cut you're going to need something familiar—besides your family—to turn toward. Do not let your separation from the service represent a separation from everything you know. Don't let the military be all you know. Join some local organizations; get active in school

and other community matters. It will give you some sense of continuity and will be your only recent "civilian" experience. You'll also make some contacts who might give you a good start toward your next career.

4. Develop as many "civilian" skills as you can before the pressure is on. This critical move is much easier if you know what you're going to be. And please remember, military expertise does not necessarily transfer directly to civilian expertise. The training and experience are valuable and will be a great help. But gear your skills to what you want to be, not what you are now.

5. Take time to evaluate. Write down your skills, goals, and requirements. Work on whittling away at your requirements. Identify intermediate objectives, and accomplish them as you go. Assess exactly where you are and where you need to go in every area discussed in this book.

6. Start your reconnaissance as early as possible, and make it detailed. Apply it to work, housing, community, and every other aspect of your transition. Never try "winging it" or going "cold turkey." Even with careful planning and preparation, you'll have enough "winging" to do.

7. Keep the entire family involved and informed. It's easy to withdraw into yourself, particularly when you've spent a career keeping your concerns to yourself and not worrying the family. You need them now. If you're too stubborn to admit that, realize they need you more than ever. You can be a big help to each other.

Moving from military to civilian life involves many major changes. If you plan to keep your thoughts straight during the process, remember that the things happening to you are happening to thousands each year. You recognize them, and therefore, you're just a step ahead of the game.

You're planning for the next third, or more, of your life. Treat it with respect, and plan properly. Seek counsel when you need it. Take courses, and keep a handle on exactly where you are in the planning process.

The Contentment Phase
★★

The "contentment phase" is really a goal. The point of this book is to help you achieve this goal. Contentment is classified as a phase because it'll hopefully take up the major part of your postmilitary life. Some people call this the "be something else" phase. Once you are something else, you've got the transition whipped. Oh, you're still authorized to get all choked up at a parade and remember the days in uniform, and rightly so. But the past is past, and it's time to look to the future!

In It Together

This chapter is designed to help the entire family make the transition from military to civilian life. The family as a whole will have many issues to deal with and will need as much help and advice as possible. This chapter is divided into three sections, each focusing on a specific aspect of your transition. Each section is followed by a simple checklist that summarizes important information you will want to remember. Keep these checklists handy so nothing will be forgotten.

Making the Move
★★★

What does *permanent* mean? This is certainly not a word military personnel and their families are familiar with. You've probably relocated at least once while in the service, so you may be wondering why this move is so special. Well, you're not in the military anymore, and hopefully this move will be a relatively permanent one. Hopefully this new location will be a place you and your family can finally call "home." It will be much easier to settle in and concentrate on making it a home if you can make the move itself as worry free as possible. This section is designed to help you and your family organize your move efficiently and effectively and to make sure you don't forget all those last-minute details.

The move affects the entire family both personally and professionally. Most people focus all their energy on moving the household and overlook the fact that they have to make a professional move as well. This may seem obvious if after leaving the military you find you must relocate to a new area to obtain a job in your desired field, but have you asked how this move may affect your spouse professionally? Again, the focus of this chapter is on relocating the entire family, not just the retired soldier, so keep in mind how each section can be applied to each family member's situation.

Relocation

Okay, you're not in the military anymore and hopefully you've been working diligently with all your resources to determine what your next step will be. It is more than likely that you will find yourself relocating to a new area, be it 30 miles or 3,000 miles away from the base that you've called home for the last part of your military service. Whether it's for personal or professional reasons and no matter how close or far the move is, it's no small undertaking. You've probably made many a move from base to base as you've been restationed during your term of service, so more than likely you're getting pretty familiar with the whole moving process. Knowing that what the Department of Defense calls a permanent change of stations (PCS) may last only eleven months, you're surely used to making a chaotic move. This move will be much more permanent, so let's concentrate on developing an approach that will make it efficient, orderly, and as stress free as possible.

Whether or not you are still in the military, you can tap into some valuable sources of information on your base. The Army Community Services (ACS), Navy and Marine Family Service Centers (FSC), and Air Force Family Support Centers (FSC) can provide you with information, referral services, programs, brochures, and workshops on everything from moving and stress management to overseas relocation and employment assistance. It's always helpful to use as many agencies as possible before you have officially left the service because you may not be eligible for some programs and workshops once you've actually retired. However, you can always call or visit the office to pick up literature and ask some questions.

Because the process can be overwhelming, it's a good idea to divide the move into some basic stages.

Stage 1: Preparing for the Move

Developing a plan of action is always a good first step. It's a good idea for you and your family to decide what you want your end result to be and design your plan for getting there accordingly. Obviously, it is easier for a single person with no house, car, or family to make the move. The more extensive your household, the more complicated the move will be and the greater the need for preplanning.

One of your biggest concerns will be housing. You will need to make the decision of whether to sell or rent your current home and to buy or rent your new one. Take the current market conditions for buying, selling, or renting a home into consideration when making your decision. You should be familiar with your local real estate market as well as the prospects in your new community. You can track the market of your new community by subscribing to the local newspaper and contacting the Chamber of Commerce in that area. Also keep in mind that if you decide to sell, you will have to invest both time and money into making repairs to your house.

A good source of information during this decision-making process is the Housing Relocation Assistance Program (HARP), which is controlled by the Corps of Engineers. It will provide you with valuable information and advice on buying and selling a home and property management. You can also find out if you are eligible for government assistance in selling your home. The housing office on your base can give you more information on this program and who to contact about it.

Part of planning ahead is taking into account the unavoidable expenses of relocation. The Finance Center on your base may be able to answer your questions about hidden expenses to be prepared for. It also may be a good idea for you and your family to set up a savings plan and budget during this period of relocation. If possible, begin saving well in advance of your move since you will most likely feel the financial impact of the temporary loss of more than one income during the move. Try to save at least one credit card just for emergencies. You're bound to run into more than one unforeseen expense as you make the move. Publications, such as "Finding and Financing a Home," put out by the USAA Foundation, will also be of value to you. Chapter 8 of this book gives you more information on how to finance this period of transition.

Make a stop at the Transportation Office on your base and pick up information packets and brochures on how to coordinate a move with a moving company and other aspects of transporting goods to and from your current and future residence.

Another avenue to explore is a relocation service. A relocation service is a national network of real estate firms whose purpose is to offer services for outgoing and incoming clients. A relocation counselor in your area can put you in contact with someone at your chosen destination. He or she can also arrange for you to work with someone who is retired from the military. This person will be able to give you the perspective of someone who has gone through the same circumstances and series of events you now find yourself in. A relocation service will give you information not only on real estate services, but also on educational, recreational, and job opportunities. For example, many have programs in which a client can prequalify for a mortgage as well as be eligible for special military discounts and services. Contact your local base housing office or look in the yellow pages for the relocation service office nearest you.

Many realtors, banks, and family centers offer "Welcome Kits" designed to help orient you and your family to a new environment. They usually include maps of the area and information on schools, medical services, recreation, shopping, and community services, as well as a list of phone numbers for utility companies. Call these companies as soon as you can. It will be nice to have electricity, phone, and water service as soon as you move in!

The local Chamber of Commerce is a good resource for answers to your questions about the area you are considering relocating to. It has numerous pamphlets, maps, and brochures about the region that should aid you in your research and decision making. You may want to request information about the following topics:

★ **Job market.** What is the unemployment rate? Is it a developing area?

★ **Housing.** What are housing costs? What are land prices in the area?

★ **Realtors.** Ask for a referral list of realtors.

★ **Cost of living.** What are school, property, and local tax rates?

★ **Recreation.** Ask for a referral list of recreation, parks, malls, and so on.

★ **Climate and environment.** What's the climate? What's the crime rate?

★ **Schools.** Ask for a referral list of schools, daycare options, and places of worship.

Stage 2: Making the Move

You've done as much preplanning as possible and now you find yourself on the road to your new home. The actual journey can be a nice family vacation as you visit sites and enjoy spending time together, or it can turn into a nightmare as people get tired and irritable traveling long distances. Plan your trip together and try to make it as tolerable for everyone as possible. Make sure your travel reservations are confirmed so you don't run into a hassle at the airport or hotel. If you are traveling with pets, find out ahead of time if the hotel/motel you'll be stopping at allows pets. If not, make arrangements with a kennel. While on the road, record your mileage and expenses to be sure you stay within your budget.

While you are traveling, you should know exactly were some important items, such as the following, are stored.

★ An inventory of possessions.

★ Real estate deeds and titles.

★ Tax papers.

★ Birth certificates, wills, medical records, and other personal papers.

★ Insurance policies, bonds, and so forth.

★ Valuables, such as jewelry, coin collections, etc.

Try to work together as a team to make the travel as safe and comfortable as possible.

Stage 3: Moving In

The move isn't complete just because you've arrived at your new destination; you still have a lot of unpacking and settling in to do. Have your inventory list on hand once you've contacted the moving company to unload your goods, so that you can check for any damaged or lost items. For your convenience, the moving company will place the items in the rooms you request. Be aware that they are responsible for reassembling any furniture they might have dismantled before the move. Put aside some of the unpacking for another time. Don't try to do everything at once.

If you weren't able to make a visit to your new community before the move, take some time to get acquainted with the area now. Locate the nearest medical facilities, banks, police station, grocery stores, and gas stations. Most importantly though, give yourselves some time to rest and work at becoming comfortable with your new community and new home.

Legal concerns. Because of the many changes that take place during relocation you will have some legal concerns that will need to be addressed. Matters that should be included on your legal to-do list include: insurance and claims, leases and real estate contracts, and banking.

★ **Insurance and claims.** You should be aware that the condition of your goods and possessions is probably not going to improve during the move, and it's very likely that it will deteriorate. Make arrangements with an insurance representative to be sure that your possessions are properly insured for the move. Be familiar with the stipulations on claims and coverage. Also, be aware that different states have different insurance laws, and you will need to attend to your automobile insurance, driver's license, and registration during your move. Your insurance agent will be able to answer your questions on these matters so you can make sure you are adequately insured.

★ **Leases and real estate contracts.** Do not hesitate to seek legal advice when signing a lease or real estate contract. You will need to be sure you understand everything you're getting into and that you read the fine print. If you don't already have a trusted and competent lawyer, do some research when locating a new one. Trusting friends, relatives, and business associates can give you good referrals.

★ **Banking.** Relocation tends to complicate your financial matters. Check with the bank that currently holds your accounts and see if it has a branch in your new area. Many times the institution can continue to provide services without any interruption if you notify a representative of your situation. If you choose to switch to a local account, you will need to close out your old accounts and open new ones. Feel free to contact the bank's service center with any questions or concerns you might have about closing and opening accounts.

There is a lot of information to remember so the following checklist summarizes the various tasks to be completed in organizing your move. Keep it on hand and refer to it during your move to make sure you don't overlook any aspect of your relocation.

☑ *Checklist for Relocation*

✔ Set aside savings for the move.

✔ Contact credit card companies; confirm expiration dates and credit limits.

✔ Make an inventory of valuable possessions.

✔ Make a list of who to notify about the move.

✔ Obtain medical, optical, and dental records.

✔ Give away or sell unwanted materials.

✔ Obtain change-of-address cards from the post office.

✔ Discontinue utility services.

✔ Return/retrieve all loaned goods.

✔ Renew prescriptions.

✔ Retrieve items being stored, repaired, cleaned, or altered.

✔ Research banks, medical facilities, schools, and child-care facilities.

✔ Research car pool/transportation options.

✔ Research activities for the entire family.

Career Move

A move forces you and your family to make many changes in your lives, and, for many, this also means a change in careers. One family member whose career could be affected by a major move is your spouse. The transition often means that a spouse will have to give up his or her current job and face temporary loss of the income and seniority he or she has earned. If you and your spouse want or need to begin working soon after the move is completed, a lot of job hunting and preparation needs to be done prior to the move. Both of you might qualify for a position with the federal government, and you can look into these opportunities by contacting the Employment Assistance Office on your base or by making a visit to your local Department of Labor office. The Employment Assistance Office can tell you what services you may still be eligible for now that you have retired from service. This office will offer resumé, cover letter, interview, and job correspondence workshops especially geared toward military personnel and their families.

You can also take advantage of the services offered by federal and state employment agencies. Job assistance is available through local state employment service offices for anyone looking for a job, though veterans are given priority. They will help you assess your skills and interests so as to match them with job descriptions provided by employers for referral. They can also give you information on apprenticeship and training programs that are available through the city, state, and federal governments. Refer to the list of state employment service agencies in each state capital included in Appendix 1. Call the number listed by your state for information on the branch office nearest to you or check in your local phone book.

The U.S. Department of Labor will be of great help to you and your spouse with the job search. The following subsections detail the services offered by this department.

Employment Counseling

When you visit the Department of Labor, you are assigned an employment counselor who will describe the services offered by the department and help you decide what paths to take and where to begin. These specially trained counselors will help you choose a field of work by talking over your interests, work experience, and training. The counselor will review your credentials and give you information on requirements and job opportunities in different career fields. If you state that you are retired from the military, you have the option of working with a counselor who is also a veteran and familiar with the challenges and opportunities unique to a soldier in transition.

Job Placement Services

The Department of Labor provides direct job-search and counseling services to individuals seeking jobs. Employers list thousands of job openings with the department and the counselors can help match your skills and career goals with these openings.

Job-Search Skills

The Department of Labor offers guides, workshops, and seminars to help you improve and develop the skills you will need to effectively market yourself. Such topics include creating a resumé, interviewing techniques, image development, and job-search strategies.

Computerized Job Searches

Many offices have self-directed job-search computer terminals called The *WORK* Station and *Jobs Plus!* These computers let you perform your own job search. The computers have an up-to-date list of all job openings listed with the Department of Labor. Often the employer contact information is displayed right on the screen, so you can contact the employer directly, or you may ask to speak with one of the office's labor service representatives for referral. The *WORK* Station and *Jobs Plus!* can also give you information on civil service examinations, the labor market, education and training, community services, other job-related services provided by the Department of Labor, department publications and video tapes, and more. It will also display a statewide directory of Department of Labor offices for your convenience.

Counseling/Testing Services and Civil Service Examinations

Not only will the counselors help you assess your job skills and work interests to find a career that's right for you, they will also use a variety of validated tests and testing techniques. Such tests include aptitude, clerical skills, literacy tests, and career interest checklists. The office can also provide you with information on state, federal, county, and city civil service examinations which the government uses to fill job openings. The many testing services available to a soldier in transition are covered in Chapter 7.

Publications

You can pick up copies of publications of interest to job seekers, such as those on unemployment insurance, job-search skills, training programs, youth programs, labor laws, and labor market information.

Training Programs

The Department of Labor has information on training programs, some of which provide funding assistance, that can help you enhance your skills and make you more valuable to a potential employer.

An example of the Training Programs available include the following:

★ **Apprentice programs.** An apprenticeship program combines on-the-job training with classroom instruction. Employers coordinate programs with the Department of Labor, which assists with the recruitment and selection of qualified individuals, like yourself.

★ **On-the-Job Training.** Like the apprenticeship programs, the Department of Labor works with employers to screen and refer candidates for on-the-job training programs conducted by the employer at the work site. These programs are funded under the Job Training Partnership Act, Chamber On-the-Job Training Programs, Skills Training Programs, and more.

★ **Training for Veterans.** The Department of Labor refers former soldiers to programs especially for veterans' training, such as programs included under the Job Training Partnership Act—Title IV and the Service Members Occupational Conversion and Training Act (SMOCTA). The latter is designed to assist veterans discharged on or after August 2, 1990, to complete the transition from military service to private sector employment by subsidizing employers' training costs. The benefits of SMOCTA are covered in more detail in Chapter 4.

Veterans' Services

The Veterans' Bill of Rights for Employment Services gives priority in referrals to jobs and training to all eligible veterans. For example, according to the bill of rights, the New York State Department of Labor's commitment to veterans is as follows:

1. To ensure that veterans are treated with courtesy and respect at all New York State Department of Labor facilities.

2. To give priority for job referrals to qualified veterans and eligible persons.

3. To give priority for training referral to qualified veterans and eligible persons.

4. To give preferential treatment to special disabled veterans in the provision of all needed local office services.

5. To provide information and effective referral assistance to veterans and eligible persons regarding needed benefits and services that may be obtained through other agencies.

Special Services

The services offered by the Department of Labor are very accessible. Most offices have evening hours for your convenience and some even provide play areas for your child. In addition, the Department has a staff of individuals specially trained in veterans services. For more information, ask to speak with the veteran's employment representative at your local Department of Labor office.

Transition Assistance Program

The Department of Labor has also designed a program especially for transitioning soldiers and their families called the Transition Assistance Program (TAP). It is applicable for every branch of the military and is designed to help the soldier in transition work through the job-search process so as to successfully transfer all military experience into a civilian career. Ask a Department of Labor counselor to explain what TAP services you may still be eligible for.

Employment Agencies

Employment agencies are a good avenue to explore because they usually specialize in particular occupations, and many times the placement fee is paid by the employer when someone is hired. However, some agencies require you to pay a registration and/or placement fee. Since you are probably operating on a reduced income at this time, you will want to locate a service where all fees are paid by the employer. You shouldn't have too much trouble finding one as there are plenty of services that operate this way.

A meeting with a representative from one of these agencies usually entails completing an application, supplying a list of references, and participating in an interview with a representative to assess your goals, skills, and experience. Some may require that you complete some skill tests, like a timed typing test. Employers list job openings with agencies who refer possible employees. It is the agency's responsibility to check your references and verify your qualifications, which is one of the reasons many employers operate their searches through such agencies. The Department of Labor will be able to refer you to some respectable agencies in your county. The yellow pages of your phone book will also have a list of private employment agencies in your area.

School or College Placement Services

Make sure to visit any schools or colleges in your area that may have a career planning office. Although some services may only be available to students and alumni, others may also be offered to the general public and should not be left unexplored. These offices usually house a fairly substantial library of books on the job-search process, such as preparing a resumé, writing effective job-search correspondence, and interviewing techniques. They will also have books that target specific careers and provide insight on how to tap into those fields. Though you may not be eligible for campus-supported programs and workshops on such topics, you can certainly contact the office and ask to use their library.

Other Resources

Other options you may use include visiting the Chamber of Commerce and looking through the telephone directory for lists of companies that correspond with your career interests. If you can get some names of individuals who are high up in these companies, you can write to them and request an information interview. If you explain your situation and simply ask to meet with that person to find out a little bit more about the field and what type of experience and education is the norm, you can learn some valuable information. Generally, people are more than willing to talk with you about their career field and how they got started. Such a meeting could give you the lead you're looking for.

If you are a member of a military association, such as American Military Retirees Association Inc. (AMRA), you are entitled to the many benefits of that organization. Many support job assistance programs and job banks specifically for retired military persons. If you aren't a member of a military association but would like more information on the services they sponsor for veterans, look up the number of the national office listed in the yellow pages of your phone book or contact your local office of the Department of Veterans' Affairs.

Like moving a household, moving a career can be very overwhelming. The following is a career move checklist for you to keep on hand when relocating. Make sure not to overlook all the job-search preparations you need to make before you move.

✔ Checklist for a Career Move

✔ Prepare your resumé as soon as you and your spouse decide to relocate.

✔ Begin your job search while you are still employed.

✔ Asks friends and relatives about possible contacts.

✔ Subscribe to newspapers in your new area and watch the classifieds.

✔ Obtain a recommendation from your present employer to include with your resumé.

✔ Contact the Chamber of Commerce, register with employment agencies, and visit the Department of Labor.

✔ Visit college placement offices, and professional organizations; secure some informational interviews.

✔ Try to establish contacts when you are visiting the area and house hunting.

Becoming Part of a New Community
★★★

Everyone will have some degree of difficulty adjusting to a new home, a new community, and a new way of life. Perhaps the one who will face the most difficulty throughout this period is your child. That's why this section is directed toward helping children adjust, although it certainly applies to the family unit as a whole. Here's a list of things you'll need to work on together as you all prepare for the changes ahead.

Team Spirit

Make sure everyone feels like a part of the team. Let everyone share in as much of the decision-making process as possible. Make sure to help each other maintain a positive attitude and share your feelings with one another—no one should feel alone. Work together to research your new area so no one will feel as if their feelings don't matter as everyone works to adapt to the new environment. As a family you are a team; work together as one and support each individual member.

Honesty

Honesty is still the best policy. Be honest with your child every step of the way. This will certainly be a traumatic time for him or her, and, if a move is required, he or she will face a lot of uncertainty. Children get stressed, anxious, and depressed too. Maintain open lines of communication with your child and try to answer any questions he or she has as truthfully as possible. Most important, let your child be involved in the move from the beginning. Respecting children's wishes and input will make them feel a part of the group.

Attitude

Try to be as positive about the changes as possible. You'll find that your child will mirror your optimistic attitude!

Time

Be patient and remember that it will take some time before this new house/apartment and community will feel like home. Give everyone time to prepare for the change and adjust to the idea of leaving. It will take each family member a different amount of time to feel comfortable with the idea, and that's natural. Let everyone adjust at their own rate. The entire process will be less stressful and traumatic for the entire family if you are all open with your feelings, especially your apprehensions. The best thing you can do for each other is listen and offer support.

Visit

If at all possible, try to pay a visit to the city or town to which you will be relocating. If it isn't possible to bring your child along, take pictures of neighborhoods, schools, parks, and any other places you can think of to show your child when you return. The move will seem less frightening if your child has a concrete image of the new area rather than leaving it a mysterious unknown. It's a good idea to allow your child some input into the selection of your new house or apartment. This will make him or her feel like a part of the entire process. If the entire family can visit the new home, it too will be less of a mystery. You might each pick your new bedrooms and come up with some imaginative ideas as to how to decorate and personalize them. Also, try to observe the other children in the neighborhood so you can get an idea of what they wear, what activities they're involved in, and anything else that will help your child fit in.

School

Children's school environment is as important to them as your job is to you. Let them have a say in the selection of the school and classes to be taken. It would be ideal if you could arrange a visit to the school and a meeting with a guidance counselor, principal, or teacher beforehand. If the child has a familiar face or two during the first week, it will seem less scary and overwhelming.

Activities

This will be an especially difficult time for your child and you will want to try and make the transition as smooth and painless as possible. Friendships and a sense of belonging are very important to adolescent children and the destruction of either may leave a lasting impression. Encouraging them to participate in new activities and organizations will help them find new interests and make new friends. Work together to research available activities that your child might be interested in joining. Try to obtain a subscription to the local paper to familiarize yourselves with the community names, sports, and recreational activities. This will give everyone a sense of belonging once they arrive and will given them something to look forward to as you prepare to move.

Don't forget yourself when researching the area! Look at the ads in the local paper to get an idea of clubs, gyms, bars, restaurants, theaters, and other recreational activities that will be important to you and your spouse.

Obstacles

If you are moving to an area where there is a significant language or cultural difference, make sure to work together to learn about these differences. You can get books and brochures about your new environment from the library. Let everyone share in the excitement of discovering new customs. You may also wish to enroll in a language class to get a head start on learning the new language. Working together to learn these things will help to alleviate your apprehensions as well as your child's. It will also remove one of the obstacles both you and your child will face in making new friends.

Stress Management—Eight Useful Steps
★★★

Whether you believe it or not, you and your family are going to suffer through a stressful period. Change and stress are almost synonymous, and if you are preparing yourselves for change, you must also prepare for stress. The following subsections list eight steps that will teach you and your family what stress is, how it affects you, and what you can do to keep it under control.

Step 1: Definition

First and foremost, you need to understand what stress is; how it affects you; and what its symptoms, signs, and effects are. Some of the elements listed may seem familiar, but you may never have recognized them as a part of stress. You wouldn't be able to go out and purchase a new car if you had no idea what a car was. The same holds true for stress. You may know that it is something that everyone gets, but never really understand what it is. Let's begin your understanding with the literal definition of stress, then we'll discuss what it really means to you and your family.

Webster's Tenth Collegiate Dictionary defines stress as follows:

> A state resulting from a stress; *esp*: one of bodily or mental tension resulting from factors that tend to alter an existent equilibrium.

Believe it or not, this is what you will experience if you aren't already. The change from soldier to civilian is going to make a big impact on your life, and that in turn is likely to create stress. Though there are some people who experience little anxiety when placed in new situations, most of us have trouble with change and need some insight in knowing how to deal with it.

Step 2: Awareness

One of the most important steps in dealing with stress is being aware that it is perfectly normal for you to experience anxiety during this period of readjustment. A lot of things in your life will be temporarily turned upside down. But remember that the situation will change, and your awareness will keep you in control. This is only temporary!

The emotional stress that arises from the loss of a job or undergoing a career change can rank right up there with the death of a loved one or a divorce. Ask anyone who has suffered through a job loss, and they'll tell you that the degree of anxiety it imposed on them was surprising. They'll probably also agree that they should have better prepared. So, if the second step is awareness, the third is preparation.

Step 3: Preparation

You have already begun preparing yourself by purchasing this book. You're reading chapters that focus on important aspects of your transition. You can certainly use the suggestions and resources outlined in this book to your advantage. By familiarizing yourself with the symptoms and effects of stress, you will be better prepared to manage them. What are the stress factors you'll need to be prepared for?

Financial Problems

Outstanding debts, loss of income, and budgeting problems are sources of stress for the entire family. Now that you are in a period of transition and readjustment, your income may not be at the level you are accustomed to. Be prepared to tighten your purse strings and work at cutting your spending level down to the bare minimum. Get the entire family to work together to create a budget that will make your income and/or savings meet all of your necessary expenditures and stretch until you are settled again. Communicating as a family and working as a team will allow everyone affected by the changes to understand the situation and the need to make sacrifices. Prepare yourself for possible financial problems.

Job Changes

Whenever you change careers, you are bound to feel anxious and stressed. Your worry will inevitably filter into the family environment and affect the whole unit. Getting the whole family involved in a job search will not only lighten the burden on your shoulders, but also create a more positive atmosphere in this time of uncertainty. Prepare yourself for the stress and time commitment of a job search.

Retirement

You may choose to take this opportunity to go into at least partial retirement. If so, you are bound to feel tension over your drastically reduced income and increased leisure time. This is a big period of readjustment; realizing this will help you become better prepared for it. Financial planning becomes vital. As for the increased leisure time, relax and enjoy it. Use this extra time! Make time for hobbies, interests, and activities with the family that you've always been interested in, but never had the time to pursue.

Family Changes

As we have said, this period of readjustment will affect your family, causing moods to change, and possible friction to arise. You will all have to deal with job changes, relocation, and possible distancing from friends and relatives. This may be especially difficult for children to handle. By keeping the lines of communication open and by working as a team, everyone will be able to get through it with as little stress as possible.

If any of these situations are coupled with personal loss, illness, or injury, you may experience stress symptoms that you aren't even aware of. Educating yourself and your family about how to recognize the symptoms of stress will make you all better prepared and able to deal with the stress in a healthy and timely fashion.

Step 4: Recognition of Anxiety

Okay, now you understand that you're facing some stressful situations and that you need to be aware and prepared. But what are the physical and mental symptoms of stress, and how do you recognize them?

One major end-product of stress is *anxiety*. Anxiety is that worried feeling you get when you fear something bad might happen. Because you are in the middle of many changes, you may be fearful and apprehensive, and you're probably holding back these thoughts and feelings to protect the ones around you. Wondering if you'll be happy in your new area, worrying about a new job, and thinking about your financial situation are all very valid fears. Some of the most common symptoms caused by anxiety are the following:

★ Nervousness

★ Trembling

★ Dizziness

★ Racing or pounding heart

★ Inability to relax

★ Increase in or loss of appetite

★ Shortness of breath

It is normal to have a certain amount of anxiety because we're always faced with new decisions, opportunities, and situations. However, if you don't learn to deal with and control your anxiety, you could find yourself facing some serious health problems, such as ulcers and high blood pressure.

Step 5: Recognition of Depression

Another by-product of stress is *depression*. Depression is an overwhelming feeling of sadness, disappointment, frustration, or hopelessness. You may feel depressed and anxious, which is perfectly normal. It's very difficult to be in complete control at all times, and allowing yourself to experience these feelings is much healthier than ignoring them. Some signs of depression to look for include the following:

★ Fatigue and loss of sleep

★ Loss of appetite

★ Lack of concentration

★ Feeling of restlessness

★ Loss of interest in daily activities

★ Feelings of sadness, disappointment, frustration, and hopelessness

It is common to experience these symptoms, but if they don't go away they may lead to physical symptoms, including headaches and weight loss. Prolonged depression is a very serious problem because it can lead to more serious problems, such as substance abuse. See your physician if your symptoms are intense and prolonged!

Step 6: Coping Strategies

If you find yourself suffering from anxiety or depression because of stress, there are many things you can do to keep the tension under control. Making use of the following suggestions will keep stress within healthy limits and allow you to focus your energy on the tasks at hand.

Be Organized!

Right now you have so many different concerns that your list of tasks may seem endless. To help relieve some of this tension, try creating a detailed plan for each of your objectives. You will save yourself valuable time and energy in the long run by creating to-do lists and prioritizing them. This will also help to avoid forgetting important responsibilities that are certain to create stress. It feels great to look at a list of crossed-off items and see how much you've accomplished.

Be Realistic!

It's impossible to do everything at the last minute and you'd have to be superhuman to do it all by yourself. Once you've prioritized your responsibilities, set realistic goals for yourself and call upon friends, family and service organizations to help you. It also helps if you can avoid undertaking more than one large project at a time.

Be Optimistic!

Go at your work with a positive attitude. Be confident that you've prepared yourself as well as possible for the upcoming challenges, and have faith in your efforts. You are more likely to be successful if you believe in yourself and your abilities.

Be Open!

When you feel stressed and overwhelmed, don't hold it in. Talk out your feelings with family or friends. Keeping your feelings bottled up is only going to make the situation worse. Let those close to you know your plans and ask for help whenever needed. The more help you recruit, the faster you'll get items crossed off your list and the more manageable your tasks will seem.

Be Good to Yourself!

Make sure to budget some free time when you can relax, exercise, or just plain take a break. Exercise is a great outlet for working off stress and boosting your energy level when you start to feel tired and frustrated. Once you've completed a task, treat yourself to something special like a night out on the town or a quiet evening alone with a good book. You also have to remember to be good to your body. It's always a good idea to visit your family physician regularly for checkups. If you find yourself suffering from physical ailments that you attribute to stress, consult your doctor. Make sure not to neglect this important point, which is easy to do when you're very busy. If you find the symptoms worsening there are many services available to assist you. Be aware of what you're feeling and don't be afraid to seek extra help.

Step 7: Getting Help

If you find that just talking to your usual confidants isn't enough support, there are many other resources you can take advantage of. Don't be too proud to ask for help; we've all had to at one time or another!

Private Physician

As mentioned earlier, your private physician can be of great help in times of stress. He or she can offer some suggestions on how to reduce anxiety levels by prescribing a balanced diet and exercise program. You will also find a lot of literature in your doctor's waiting area that may contain additional suggestions on ways to reduce stress and maintain a healthy body when under pressure.

Clergy

Religious organizations usually offer support workshops and programs tailored to coping with emotional stress. In addition, most clergy are qualified counselors and are trained to help people deal with personal problems, including stress management. They should also be able to help you locate additional support services in your area.

Counselors and Therapists

The counseling/therapy field is growing in response to the demands of people like yourself who need some outside help and consultation. You should have no problem finding a counselor, family therapist, psychologist, or psychiatrist in your area who will meet your needs. Be aware, however, that these services can be costly. Make sure you do your research when selecting professional help.

Military Resources

Even though you are no longer in the military, you may still be able to tap into many of the resources offered. Make another visit to the transition office on your base and find out what services you are still eligible for. Your local branch of the Veterans' Affairs office will be able to point you in the right direction.

Crisis Intervention Centers

These centers usually post hotline numbers so services can be used 24 hours a day. If you feel you need emergency help, do not hesitate to call these numbers. They are located in the yellow pages of your local phone book, or the operator can provide directory assistance. Crisis intervention centers offer individual counseling sessions and can give you information for referrals.

Step 8: Keeping Your Sense of Humor

If you maintain your sense of humor, even when everything else seems to go wrong, you'll have something to fall back on. The following was published by the Canadian Association of Labour Media as a humorous list of ways to handle stress.

1. Jam tiny marshmallows up your nose and try to sneeze them out.

2. Use your Mastercard to pay your Visa bill.

3. Pop some popcorn without putting the lid on.

4. When someone says, "Have a nice day," tell them you have other plans.

5. During your next meeting, sneeze, and then loudly suck the phlegm down your throat.

6. Make a list of all the things you have already done.

7. Dance naked in front of your pets.

8. Put your toddler's clothes on backwards and send him or her to preschool as if nothing were wrong.

9. Go shopping; buy everything; sweat in them; return them the next day.

10. Drive to work in reverse.

11. Read the dictionary backward and look for subliminal messages.

12. Start a rumor and see if you recognize it when it gets back to you.

13. Bill your doctor for the time you spend in his or her waiting room.

14. Get a box of condoms, then wait in line at the checkout counter and ask the cashier where the fitting rooms are.

Of course it's not recommended that you actually do any of these (for obvious reasons, such as possible physical injury—it'd be pretty uncomfortable having marshmallows shoved up your nose), but the list lets you bring a little humor into every situation. Find a place to post the list, like on your refrigerator or bathroom mirror, anywhere that will catch your attention and give you a humorous boost.

Keep the eight steps of stress management in mind:

1. Definition

2. Awareness

3. Preparation

4. Recognition of Anxiety

5. Recognition of Depression

6. Coping Strategies

7. Getting Help

8. Keeping Your Sense of Humor

Now that you've educated yourself and your family as to the signs, effects, and treatments of stress, you're ready to take on any obstacle successfully and relatively tension free.

Financing the Transition

If you are anything like the millions of Americans whose favorite pastime is to consume, consume, consume, you've probably already been in the position of having your spending outweigh your income. Many people find themselves in need of financial planning, but it will be even more important for you and your family because you are facing a change in your employment. This change may mean that you will have to deal with a period of unemployment. Be realistic and plan for the worst. That way you won't find yourself unprepared. It is very likely that you will have to make cuts in your spending to safeguard against overextending yourself during this period of transition. This chapter is dedicated to helping you plan for a transition that won't break you financially. Learn to use all available resources and take advantage of the benefits and opportunities to which your time in the service has entitled you.

The first step is to assess what your income and spending total and learn to budget accordingly.

Preliminary Planning
★★★

When preparing your financial plan, you will need to do the following:

1. Compute your current financial status.

2. Decide on long and short-range financial goals.

Next, you will want to figure out how much money you will have coming in each month, then list all your anticipated monthly expenses. The following worksheets will help you determine if you will need to supplement your income during the transition.

It's a good idea to complete two financial budget worksheets: one to estimate your budget prior to the transition and the other to estimate your budget for an average month following the transition. You will want to use your income immediately after you leave the service to reduce debts and increase savings to cover any periods of unemployment. Be realistic with your estimates and don't forget to include the following:

★ Housing

★ Utilities

★ Transportation

★ Medical and dental insurance

★ State and local taxes

These worksheets should give you a good idea of how long your savings will stretch before you have to find employment and will also help determine the salary you will need to make at your next job.

Financial Budget Worksheet

Monthly Budget

1. **Housing**
   Rent or mortgage _____
   Maintenance _____
   Heating _____
   Electricity _____
   Water _____
   Telephone _____
   Other (cable, etc.) _____
   Subtotal _____

2. **Food**
   Groceries _____
   Restaurant meals _____
   Other _____
   Subtotal _____

3. **Transportation**
   Car maintenance _____
   Public
     transportation _____
   Gas _____
   Other _____
   Subtotal _____

4. **Personal**
   Laundry _____
   Personal grooming _____
   Clothes _____
   Recreation _____
   Membership dues _____
   Other _____
   Subtotal _____

5. **Child Care**
   Day care/babysitter _____
   School fees _____
   Allowances _____
   Other _____
   Subtotal _____

6. **Debts**
   Credit cards _____
   Loans _____
   Other _____
   Subtotal _____

continued

7. **Insurance**   Dental and medical _____
    Personal and life _____
    Car _____
    Home _____
    Other _____
    Subtotal _____

8. **Medical**   Doctor _____
    Dentist _____
    Prescriptions _____
    Other _____
    Subtotal _____

9. **Taxes**   Property tax _____
    Income tax _____
    Other _____
    Subtotal _____

10. **Miscellaneous**   Entertainment _____
    Subscriptions _____
    Job search _____
    Education _____
    Other _____
    Subtotal _____

    Total _____

Financial Planning Worksheet

1. Total amount of savings you currently have _____

2. Total amount of additional savings you will accumulate prior to or immediately after leaving the service _____

3. Total amount of last paycheck _____

4. Total amount of additional savings you will accumulate from sale of property or goods _____

   Total of Lines 1 through 5   **(A)** _____

6. Total amount of money you will withdraw from savings to pay debts or allowances _____

7. Total amount of money you will withdraw from savings to pay for moving and relocation costs _____

8. Total amount of money you will withdraw from savings for housing and travel costs _____

   Total of Lines 6 through 8   **(B)** _____

   Subtract Line B from Line A (This is the amount of money you will have to live on during the transition.)   **(9)** _____

   Total amount of monthly expenses for an average month following transition (This number comes from your second worksheet.)   **(10)** _____

   Divide Line 9 by Line 10 (This is an estimate of the number of months you can go without finding a job.)   **(11)** _____

Important Terms

If this is the first time you've prepared your own financial plan, you may be feeling overwhelmed by the terms, language, and lingo used by business professionals. The following list of definitions will help you become familiar with the terms you come across during your planning.

Accounts payable: Outstanding bills to be paid at a future time.

Annuity: An investment that doesn't generate a taxable income as long as it remains an annuity. Fixed annuities are guaranteed a fixed interest rate for one year. This is usually an investment with an insurance company.

Assets: Things you own, like your home, car, real estate, and other valuables.

Bond: A type of security issued by a company or government unit that borrows your money and pays you a fixed interest rate. Each bond has a specific redemption date but can be redeemed earlier than that. After the bond is issued, its current value depends on the current interest rates offered by new bonds.

Certificate of deposit (CD): An account issued by a bank when it borrows your money for a specified period of time and pays you a fixed interest rate on it.

Dividend: Money paid to shareholders from earnings or interest through stock, a mutual fund, or a money fund.

Equity: Total assets minus total liabilities.

Individual retirement account (IRA): An account that meets government regulations for individual investment of money for retirement. The money invested does not generate any taxable income as long as it is in the IRA.

Liabilities: Debts you owe, such as on a mortgage or credit cards.

Mutual fund: A managed portfolio that sells shares of its own portfolio. This may include stocks, bonds, and money market investments.

Net worth: The total amount that remains when liabilities are subtracted from assets.

Return on capital: Money paid to you as total or partial repayment of money you have invested. This is a nontaxable payment.

Security: A single investment that has a value and a share price.

Stock: Ownership in a company, sold in units called shares.

Treasury bill (T-bill): A popular six-month bond sold by the U.S. government.

Where to Go for Help

★★★

If you haven't already, make sure to visit the following offices on your base to find out more about benefits and programs that you may qualify for now that you are a veteran. Even if you are not eligible for their programs and workshops, you can still ask to meet with a representative to ask some questions and pick up some publications and pamphlets that are available. Staff can also further explain the terms listed above.

Community Services Office

This office offers seminars and workshops to help you understand and organize your financial future. Topics covered usually include insurance, credit, consumer rights and obligations, taxes, and investments. It also provides guidance in setting up budgets and spending plans for you and your family. Contact a representative from this office to find out if you are still eligible to attend these seminars and workshops. If not, ask to meet with a representative to ask questions on those topics. You will want to find out about insurance plans especially geared for veterans and get referrals for investment planners near you.

Finance and Accounting Office

Make an appointment with a representative from this office to go over your entitlements and obligations from the military. He or she can also inform you of any educational benefits you might qualify for and help you update your tax and loan status.

Medical Office

A visit to the medical office is important in understanding what benefits carry over to you as a civilian. Staff will help you understand civilian life insurance and assist you in locating the proper medical facilities in your new community if you require ongoing treatment or have special needs.

Legal Services Office

This office provides counseling on creating a will, power of attorney, and any legal problems you may have. Services are available for matters such as the following:

★ Debtor/creditor suits

★ Landlord/tenant negotiations

★ Family law

★ Taxes

★ Appeal against type of discharge

★ Claims against the government

Contact a representative from this office to find out what services are still available to you. If he or she is unable to provide you with direct counseling, ask to be referred to a respectable law office in your area.

Local State Employment Services Office

Contact this office to learn what unemployment benefits and compensation you are entitled to while looking for new employment. Be sure to inquire about any time limits involved.

Social Security Office

Social security is a government insurance program. Almost everyone who is employed is covered by social security. A percentage of your wages has been taken out of every paycheck for this program, and you are entitled to certain benefits based on your average monthly earnings and the number of years that are credited to you. A visit to this office will inform you of the benefits for which you might qualify. You will also want to obtain the latest edition of the *Guide to Social Security and Medicare,* which is published by

William M. Mercer, Incorporated
1500 Meidinger Tower
Louisville, Kentucky 40202-3415

Certified Public Accountants

Certified public accountants are available for consultation on money management, tax preparation, and overall financial planning. They will help you understand what your resources are and how to go about managing them. Ask the Finance and Accounting Office on your base, as well as your friends and family, for a list of referrals. You will also find them listed in the yellow pages of your local phone book.

Local Banks

A representative from your local bank can give you advice on strategic investment planning including IRAs and money market accounts. It will also be to your advantage to discuss personal loan options if you think you'll need additional financial support during your transition.

Summary of Veteran's Benefits
★★★

An important aspect of financial planning is understanding and using the benefits you are entitled to as a veteran. Veterans' benefits are administered by the Department of Veterans' Affairs (VA) and are services to which you and, in some cases, your family, are entitled once you have left the military. According to the VA publication *Federal Benefits for Veterans and Dependents* (1993 edition), benefits include the following:

★ Compensation to service-disabled veterans

★ Educational assistance

★ Vocational rehabilitation

★ Home loans

★ Life insurance programs

★ Medical and dental treatment

★ Other programs

The following divisions of the Veterans' Affairs Office are the ones you will most likely deal with while doing your financial planning:

VA Regional Offices: The VA regional offices process and administer claims for VA benefits, including disability compensation, pensions, home loan guarantees, life insurance, education and training, and burial allowances.

VA Medical Center Admissions Offices: The VA medical center admissions office provides information on all types of medical care, including long-term care (nursing homes), dental care, drug and alcohol dependency, and readjustment counseling.

For more information regarding your benefits, contact your nearest VA regional office.

Exhibit 4.1 will give you an idea of what's available to you as a veteran. The Department of Veterans' Affairs publishes an annual list of veterans' benefits titled *Federal Benefits for Veterans and Dependents*. You can obtain a copy from your nearest Veterans' Affairs Office; it will be a valuable resource to you during your financial planning.

EXHIBIT 4.1

Veterans Benefits Timetable

90 days

Reemployment: You may apply to your former employer for reemployment.

Limited time

Unemployment compensation: The purpose of unemployment compensation is to give you a weekly income to meet your basic needs while searching for employment. Unemployment compensation is only available for a designated period of time. The amount and duration of payments are governed by federal and state laws and vary from state to state and case to case. Benefits are paid from federal funds. Apply at your nearest local State Employment Service/Job Service Office (*not* the VA) immediately after leaving the service. You will need to present your DD 214 form so that your eligibility for benefits can be determined. Check the yellow pages for the nearest office.

120 days

Veterans' Group Life Insurance (VGLI): Soldiers' Group Life Insurance (SGLI) may be converted to a five-year nonrenewable term policy known as Veterans' Group Life Insurance. Coverage can be obtained in increments of $10,000 up to a maximum of $200,000. This insurance is administered by the Office of Servicemen's Group Life Insurance, 213 Washington St., Newark, NJ 07102, and is available to

★ individuals being released from active duty after August 1, 1974;

★ reservists who suffer a disability while performing active duty or inactive duty for training for a period of less than 31 days; and

★ members of the Individual Ready Reserve (IRR) and Inactive National Guard (ING).

continued

This insurance program became available on August 1, 1974, and new issues are still being taken. Contact the Office of Servicemen's Group Life Insurance for further stipulations.

1 year

GI insurance: Life insurance is available for veterans with service-connected disabilities. Veterans who are totally disabled may apply for a waiver of premiums on these policies. Coverage is available up to $10,000. Contact your local VA office for more information.

Supplemental insurance: Veterans who are under the age of 65, are eligible for waiver of premiums, and have Service Disabled Veterans' Insurance may qualify for an additional $20,000 insurance policy. No waiver will be granted on the additional insurance. Contact your local VA office for more information.

10 years

Education: You may be eligible for educational assistance if you participated in either the Post-Vietnam Era Veterans' Educational Assistance Program (VEAP) (Chapter 32) or the Montgomery GI Bill (Chapter 30) while on active duty; if you had entitlement under the Vietnam Era GI Bill (Chapter 34) remaining on December 31, 1989, and were on active duty from October 19, 1984, through June 30, 1988; or if you were on active duty from October 19, 1984, through June 30, 1987, and subsequently entered into the Selected Reserve under a four-year enlistment. For members of the Montgomery GI Bill-Selected Reserve (Chapter 106), benefits end on the date of separation from the Selected Reserve or 10 years after the date eligibility began, whichever comes first. Contact your local VA office for more information.

continued

12 years	**Vocational rehabilitation:** If you are a disabled veteran, the VA, as part of a program of rehabilitation, will pay your tuition, fees, books, tools, and other program expenses, as well as a monthly living allowance, for a vocational rehabilitation program. Once you have completed the program, the department will assist you in finding employment. Contact your local VA office for more information.
No limit	**GI home loans:** The VA will guarantee your loan for the purchase of a home, farm with residence, manufactured home, or condominium. Contact your local VA office for more information.

How to Apply for Your Benefits

Eligibility for most VA benefits is based on discharge from active military service under other than dishonorable conditions. When you are discharged from service the military issues you a military discharge form known as a DD 214. This form states the type of discharge you received, such as honorable or dishonorable. If you enlisted in the military after September 7, 1980, and/or were a commissioned officer or entered active service after October 16, 1981, you must have completed two years of active duty to be eligible for VA benefits.

If you don't have the following documents on hand, request new copies, because you will need them when applying for benefits:

★ Veterans DD 214 form

★ Birth certificate

★ Marriage license

★ Medical documents

★ Training record

★ Education experience record

To file a claim, contact a Veterans' Benefit Counselor at the nearest VA regional office. If you have difficulty locating one, there should be a number in your telephone book listed under United States Government. Make sure to take along all the materials listed here and feel free to ask questions about the different benefits. This will be a semi-lengthy process as there is a substantial amount of paperwork to be completed and filed.

Remember that benefits change! New benefits may be added. For the most recent benefit list, contact your nearest VA office and request the current benefits publication. Consult your local telephone directory under United States Government, Department of Veterans' Affairs, or directory assistance for the toll-free number to reach a VA representative in all 50 states, Washington, DC, and Puerto Rico.

More Federal Benefits
★★

There are many other benefits available to veterans and their families other than those administered by the Department of Veterans' Affairs. The following sections summarize other avenues available to you and how to obtain more information about them.

Reemployment Rights

Under the Veterans' Re-employment Rights (VRR) law, a person who left a civilian job to enter active duty in the armed forces, either voluntarily or involuntarily, may be entitled to return to his or her civilian job after discharge or release from active duty. The Department of Labor administers the VRR law and the eligibility criteria include the following:

1. You must have been employed in an "other than temporary" civilian job.

2. You must have left the civilian job for the purpose of entering military service.

3. You must not remain on active duty longer than four years, unless the period beyond four years (up to an additional year) is "at the request and for the convenience of the Federal Government," and your DD 214 carries this statement.

4. You must be discharged or released from active duty "under honorable conditions."

If you meet these criteria, you may be entitled to either a better or lesser job with your civilian employer than the one you left. The main point of the VRR law is to place the returning veteran in the job that would have been attained if they had remained continuously employed instead of going on active duty. You may be entitled to benefits generally based on seniority, like pensions, pay increases, missed promotions, and missed transfers.

When you apply for reemployment make sure to keep a record of when and to whom you give the application. This is very important if you have problems attaining reemployment because you may be entitled to have the Department of Labor represent you. If you have questions on the VRR law, you can contact the Department of Labor's Director for Veterans' Employment and Training (DVET).

Veterans' Administration Disability Compensation

You are required to file your claim for this compensation as soon as you leave the service, and you will be asked to take a physical examination. Be aware that the processing can take up to six months. Benefit amounts are changed annually by Congress. The payment is distributed in monthly increments. According to the Department of Veterans' Affairs publication *Federal Benefits for Veterans and Dependents* (1993 edition), the monthly disability compensation rates are as follows:

Disability	Compensation Rate
10%	$ 85
20	162
30	247
40	352
50	502
60	632
70	799
80	924
90	1,040
100	1,730

You cannot receive both a disability check and a retirement check. The amount of your VA disability compensation will be deducted from your retirement check.

The Montgomery GI Bill

According to the pamphlet "Summary of Educational Benefits" published by the VA, educational benefits are provided for under the Montgomery GI Bill–Active Duty Educational Assistance Program. You may be eligible for educational benefits as a veteran or service person if your active duty fits into one of the following categories.

Category 1

You entered active duty for the first time after June 30, 1985, and served continuously for three years. However, only two years of active duty are required if

★ You are now on active duty,

★ You originally enlisted for two years, or

★ You have an obligation to serve four years in the Selected Reserve (you must enter the Selected Reserve within one year of your release from active duty).

In this category, your military pay must have been reduced by $100 a month for the first 12 months of active duty. You may also be eligible if you meet the following conditions:

★ You were on active duty between December 1, 1988, and June 30, 1989.

★ You withdrew your election not to participate.

★ You had your military pay reduced by $100 a month.

★ You completed the period of active duty you were obligated to serve on December 1, 1988.

Category 2

You had remaining entitlement under the Vietnam Era GI Bill on December 31, 1989; you were on active duty from October 19, 1984, to June 30, 1988, or June 30, 1987; and you served four years in the Selected Reserve after release from active duty. You must have entered the Selected Reserve within 1 year of your release from active duty.

You must have obtained a high school diploma or an equivalency certificate before December 31, 1989. Completing 12 hours towards a college degree meets the requirement.

Category 3

You were on active duty on September 30, 1990, and elected to participate in Chapter 30 before being involuntarily separated after February 2, 1991. In this category, you must have your military pay reduced by $1,200. You must have a high school diploma or equivalency. If not, you must complete the requirements for a high school diploma or its equivalency after you have been separated from active duty, but before you apply for benefits. Completing 12 hours toward a college degree meets the requirements.

To qualify, you must have received an honorable discharge. You have 36 months of entitlement under this program. If you did not complete your enlistment period, you earn only one month of entitlement for each month of active duty after June 30, 1985. You may also earn one month of entitlement for every four months spent in the Selected Reserve after June 30, 1985. You can earn a maximum of 36 months under this program. Benefits end ten years from the date of your last discharge or release from active duty.

According to the VA publication *Federal Benefits for Veterans and Dependents,* you are also eligible for the following educational and training programs with the Montgomery GI Bill:

★ You may take college courses toward associate, bachelor, or graduate degrees.

★ You may take courses toward a certificate or diploma from a business, technical, or vocational school.

★ You may be allowed to enroll in apprenticeship or on-the-job training programs.

★ You may be allowed to take correspondence courses.

For more information on the benefits you are entitled to under the Montgomery GI Bill, contact your regional VA office. All information presented here was obtained from the VA publication "Summary of Educational Benefits under the Montgomery GI Bill—Active Duty Educational Assistance Program Chapter 30 of Title 38 U.S. Code" (January 1992).

GI Loans

This is a program that lends you money to buy, build, improve, or refinance a home. You must have an honorable discharge. If you have a service-connected disability, you are automatically eligible. When you are discharged, a certificate of eligibility will be mailed to your home by the Veterans' Administration.

Loan Repayment Program (LRP)

According to *Counselor's Guide to Military Guidance Resources,* for a three- or four-year enlistment, the military pays off federally insured student loans made after October 1, 1975. The loan cannot be in default, and the individual must meet certain qualifications. Each year, the military will repay $1,500 or $33\frac{1}{3}\%$ of an eligible student loan or an outstanding principal loan balance, whichever is greater, up to $55,000. When a loan balance exceeds $55,000, $33\frac{1}{3}\%$ of $55,000 will be paid for three years.

Student Loan Repayment Program (SLRP)

For Reserve enlistments, the SLRP provides repayment of federally unsecured student loans made after October 1, 1975. The loan cannot be in default, and the individual must meet certain qualifications. Each year, a certain portion of the loan will be repaid. For an individual who enlists for a critical skill, $20,000 is repaid. For most enlistments, $10,000 of a student loan is repaid.

More about Veterans Group Life Insurance

Veterans Group Life Insurance is a low-cost life insurance program. If you were discharged on or after December 1, 1981, you are eligible for the expanded coverage that previously existed under the Servicemen's Group Life Insurance. Individuals separated before December 1, 1981, are not entitled to expanded coverage. The maximum coverage is $35,000. If you are 34 or under, the cost is $0.17 per $1,000. If you are 35 or over, the cost is $0.34 per $1,000. This coverage lasts for five years, and, although it is not renewable, it can be converted to a civilian policy at standard rates. You will not be required to take a physical or provide any proof of good health. If you participate in this program, the Office of Servicemen's Group Life Insurance will let you know within a reasonable amount of time when your policy will expire.

Employment Benefits

As a retiring veteran you are entitled to benefits that will help you find employment. If you visit the Department of Labor, they can describe the employment benefits you qualify for in detail. They also provide extensive job-search assistance especially geared for veterans.

You still qualify for benefits if you apply for federal employment. The employment benefits are in the form of points. The point system differentiates between veterans and civilians who apply for the same job at the same time, and veterans are given priority. If you served in a war between January 31, 1955, and October 15, 1976, and were awarded a campaign medal for that service, you are also eligible. If you have a service-connected disability and received the Purple Heart, you will receive additional priority.

Conclusion
★★★

By knowing your income, expenses, and benefits, and being aware that no matter how much you plan there will always be hidden costs involved with making a transition, you are well on your way to enjoying a transition from the military that won't take more of a toll on your wallet than absolutely necessary. Work together as a family to come up with a plan that will make everyone happy. Make sure to use all your resources when planning, and don't forget to include all of your benefits in your financial plan. You've certainly earned them!

The Importance of Goal Setting

Unless you focus your goals and act on them, there can be no growth or change in your life. Focus on your dreams and go after them. Build a new you. Practice the following ten methods of focusing on your dreams and goals:

1. See yourself beyond your present circumstances. Visualize what you want.

2. Ignore the negative self-talk and turn up the volume on positive thinking. Tell yourself, "I'm doing *great*!" several times a day.

3. Increase your sense that you *deserve* your dream.

4. Invest in a personal development library with books that will motivate you, particularly biographies of those who have endured hardship, persevered, and then lived their dreams (such as Helen Keller, Henry Ford, Gandhi, and Martin Luther King, Jr.).

5. Assess yourself. Get to know your strong points and the things you should work on.

6. Demand more from yourself. Don't hold back. You've got plenty of energy; use it before you lose it.

7. Take risks.

8. Stand up for what you want, don't let anyone deter you from pursuing your dreams.

9. Surround yourself with supportive, quality people.

10. Commit yourself to being unstoppable. Remember you can always have more and do more, because you can always *be* more!

Guidelines for Personal Growth
★★

The following guidelines about personal growth may be helpful as you work your way through this chapter.

★ Personal goal setting is a process of systematically growing as a person while working toward specific purposes in your life.

★ Personal growth involves changes in attitudes and behaviors that are related to your self-concept and your needs.

★ Personal growth may be possible in all areas of your life. Heredity or strong early environmental forces may hinder even desirable changes. This fact need not be demotivating, though; it simply means that you should not put unrealistic demands on yourself. To do so would divert your energies from those goals that you *can* realistically accomplish.

★ If you have certain habits, attitudes, and opinions that reduce your receptiveness to alternative ways of thinking and acting, they may keep you from changing and growing in the ways you would like. Keep an open mind as you work through the process of creating your future; try not to be limited by the boundaries of your current situation.

★ If you have defensive behavior patterns, they may deter your change and growth by distorting reality.

★ Personal growth may be accelerated by attitudes and behaviors marked by openness, receptiveness to new experiences, curiosity, risk taking, eagerness, lack of fear, and experimentation.

★ We human beings are incredibly complex; we differ in our degrees of self-understanding as well as in our levels and kinds of aspirations. Nevertheless, most of us desire some sort of personal growth.

★ Generally we tend to underestimate our abilities and our potential for accomplishment and personal growth.

This chapter provides a simple structure for creating your future through personal growth and development.

Setting Your Goals

★★

Service life is so all-encompassing that there is a great tendency to treat the end of it as the end of life itself. Ask an active duty friend about his or her goals. Chances are you'll hear, "I'd like to make colonel before I retire," or "If I can make it to E9 by the time I'm 42, I'll feel I've done well." Suppose both succeed, then retire. They have a right to be proud, and their military retirement checks will reflect their grade. Now what?

If one sets a goal, achieves it at 40 or 45, then steps into an entirely new environment with no further goals or direction, the accomplishment becomes hollow. There is an irresistible urge to live in the past, which soon wears thin with everyone except those in the same situation. Most of us need goals, and stepping into civilian life without them is asking for trouble.

Set some specific goals (always keeping in mind the question, "What am I going to be?") and shoot for them as early as possible while you're still on active duty. You can orient a job search if you know what you want to do. Deciding where you want to live becomes much easier if you know what you're going to do for a living. Doing it backwards might be troublesome later. If you pick a spot just because you like it, what about your life's work? Once you've moved, will you be able to pursue that work in the location you've chosen? If not, you have a tough and expensive relocation decision on the horizon.

Most obvious of all is the fact that you must select your career field before you can prepare for it. Once you determine your goal, you can slant education, off-duty activity, preference statements, and perhaps even duty assignments in that direction. There's absolutely nothing wrong with that, so long as "it doesn't interfere with the mission."

One of the greatest strengths of the exercises in this chapter is that they help explore ten critical areas of your life, one area at a time. These ten critical areas reflect the roles we play in various facets of our lives.

★ **Personal**. This category helps you focus on and develop goals that relate to your relationship to yourself: improving your self-image, enhancing your creative and intellectual abilities, and shifting toward a more positive attitude.

★ **Health**. This category helps you focus on and develop goals related to diet, fitness, addictions, and physical appearance.

★ **Recreation**. This category focuses on developing goals related to adding new dimensions and diversity to your lifestyle.

★ **Family**. This category is concerned with goals related to beginning, strengthening, clarifying, and enhancing your relationships with your mate or lover, children, siblings, and parents.

★ **Friendship**. This category deals with goals related to deepening and balancing relationships with old friends and building new friendships.

★ **Community**. This category helps you focus on and develop goals related to your social responsibilities and local and global communities.

★ **Career**. This category relates to goals concerning your vocation, paid or unpaid. While the term *career* too often implies paid professional activity, this book takes a broader view. The parent who stays home specifically to care for and educate children is practicing a career that is equal in importance to that of a pediatric surgeon.

★ **Financial**. This category focuses on developing goals related to your present and future material wealth and satisfaction.

★ **Household**. This category deals with goals related to the maintenance and enhancement of what may well be your largest material investment.

★ **Spiritual**. This category emphasizes goals related to the foundation on which you build peace of mind and heart.

Setting your goals is not a job you can tackle while operating on "automatic pilot." It requires careful examination, judgment, and adjustment of the various factors that make up your life.

The purpose of the following exercises is to enable you to *decide* exactly what you want in every area of your life and then help you *achieve* it. A central theme of *Out of Uniform* is that you can have everything you want, as long as you know what it is. Clarity is essential. People are failures in life, not because they lack ability or opportunity, but because they lack *clarity* about goals and the means to accomplish them.

At the start of this exercise, you are asked to think through your goals for several areas of your life. You will then be asked to prioritize your goals, organizing them in order of importance to you. In each case, ask yourself, "What do *I* really want? What are my *real* goals in life?"

With your goals clearly before you, you are asked to select your *most important goal*—the one goal that, when you achieve it, will enable you to achieve many of your other goals as well. You also are asked to think about ten ways to achieve your major goals.

You will become a more skilled thinker with every word you write, with every idea you generate, with every bit of intense, thoughtful effort you put into writing and rewriting your goals. Hard, systematic work is necessary, and self-discipline is required. Continuous action toward your goals must take place every day.

What is the pay-off? You will take complete charge of your life and turn yourself into an unstoppable, goal-achieving personality. Your self-confidence and self-esteem will increase daily. Your self-image will improve, and your ability to persist in the face of adversity will grow. You will become more focused, directed, and channeled, like a mighty river, moving forward over all obstacles to create the kind of life that you desire.

Goal Setting Exercises

1. Write out your three most important goals in life right now.
   _____
   _____
   _____

2. How would you spend your time, where would you go, what would you do, if you found out today that you had only six months to live?
   _____
   _____
   _____
   _____

3. What would you do differently if you won $1 million cash, tax free, tomorrow?
   _____
   _____
   _____
   _____

4. What have you always wanted to do but been afraid to attempt?
   _____
   _____
   _____

5. What do you enjoy doing most in life? If you could engage in any full-time activity without pay, what would it be?
   _____
   _____
   _____

6. How much money would you like to be earning
   in one year? .... $_____
   in two years? .... $_____
   in three years? .... $_____
   in four years? .... $_____
   in five years? .... $_____

7. How much do you want to be worth by the time you retire?
   $_____

8. Who else is earning the kind of money you want to earn?
   _____
   _____

continued

9. What is he or she doing differently than you that enables him or her to earn this kind of money?

_____

_____

_____

10. What are your top three personal goals?
    A. _____
    B. _____
    C. _____

11. What are your top three health goals?
    A. _____
    B. _____
    C. _____

12. What are your top three recreation goals?
    A. _____
    B. _____
    C. _____

13. What are your top three family goals?
    A. _____
    B. _____
    C. _____

14. What are your top three friendship goals?
    A. _____
    B. _____
    C. _____

15. What are your top three community goals?
    A. _____
    B. _____
    C. _____

16. What are your top three career goals?
    A. _____
    B. _____
    C. _____

17. What are your top three financial goals?
    A. _____
    B. _____
    C. _____

continued

18. What are your top three household goals?
    A. _____
    B. _____
    C. _____

19. What are your top three spiritual goals?
    A. _____
    B. _____
    C. _____

20. Based on these exercises, what do you think should be your most important goal? Your major definite purpose? Write it out in detail.

    _____
    _____
    _____
    _____
    _____
    _____

21. Now go back through your goals on the previous pages and rank them as: "A" = very important; "B" = important; and "C" = nice, but not important. Write all of your "A" goals below:

                                                        Order

     1. _____ _____
     2. _____ _____
     3. _____ _____
     4. _____ _____
     5. _____ _____
     6. _____ _____
     7. _____ _____
     8. _____ _____
     9. _____ _____
    10. _____ _____

    In the right-hand column, organize your goals from 1 (most important) to 10 (least important). This will give you a complete goal list, organized by priority.

    Select your three most important goals and write out ten things you could start doing immediately to make them realities.

continued

Goal Number One: _____

_____

	Action Steps	**Order**
1.	_____	_____
2.	_____	_____
3.	_____	_____
4.	_____	_____
5.	_____	_____
6.	_____	_____
7.	_____	_____
8.	_____	_____
9.	_____	_____
10.	_____	_____

Goal Number Two: _____

_____

	Action Steps	**Order**
1.	_____	_____
2.	_____	_____
3.	_____	_____
4.	_____	_____
5.	_____	_____
6.	_____	_____
7.	_____	_____
8.	_____	_____
9.	_____	_____
10.	_____	_____

Goal Number Three: _____

_____

	Action Steps	**Order**
1.	_____	_____
2.	_____	_____
3.	_____	_____
4.	_____	_____
5.	_____	_____
6.	_____	_____
7.	_____	_____
8.	_____	_____
9.	_____	_____
10.	_____	_____

Testing Your Goals

1. Desire: Do you really want it? _____
_____

2. Belief: Is it believable and achievable? _____
_____

3. Write it down: Is it measurable? _____
_____

4. Analyze: Where are you starting from? _____
_____

5. Determine: How will you personally benefit from achieving it? _____
_____

6. Timing: What is the deadline on your goal? _____
_____

7. Ask: What obstacles must you overcome? _____
_____

8. Research: What additional information will you require? _____
_____

9. Whose assistance or cooperation do you need? What key people are
needed? _____
_____

Planning for Your Future

Few of us would ever experience significant victories or successes without systematically planning to do so. The same is true for career transition. Success is not accidental. You can win only through preparation and implementation of good career planning. Those who fail to plan, plan to fail in their transition.

★ ★ ★ ★ ★

If I had my life to live over, I would start barefoot earlier in the spring and stay that way later in the fall. I would go to more dances. I would ride more merry-go-rounds. I would pick more daisies.
Nadine Stair (age 85)

★ ★ ★ ★ ★

How easy it is to look back on life and think about what we would have done differently, to speculate how the past would have been different had we known more or planned more. Opportunities for systematic and informed career planning were not available for many of us years ago, so we need to compensate. Occupational choice can't be left to chance. Said another way, Victor Frankel wrote, "Man does not simply exist, but always decides what his existence will be, what he will become in the next moment." We decide, we plan, we act—we are responsible.

Your life planning needs a set of guiding principles. As Stephen Covey said,

"Principles are like compasses: They are always pointing the way. And if we know how to read them, we won't get lost, confused, or fooled by conflicting voices and values." We need such guiding principles as a basis for making both short- and long-term plans and decisions.

Life planning needs an exact blueprint or action map.

> "At the fork in the road, Alice asked the Cheshire Cat which road to take? The Cheshire Cat asked, "Where do you want to go?" To which Alice replied, "I don't know." "Then," said the Cat, "It doesn't matter much which way you go."
>
> *Alice in Wonderland*

How does one plan for success? What are the structures, guidelines, and pitfalls?

The following sections provides a form to help you to begin structuring your career plan. This form should be used in conjunction with Chapter 5 which allows you to develop the goals that need to be used in your planning. Once this form is filled out, the answers may serve as complete notes that will be useful before, during, and after the interview process.

We all plan differently because our styles, needs, and demands are different. Nonetheless, we all need a plan. Use the next few pages to help with your first draft.

Tentative Career Plan

I. Factors to Consider

   A. What are your personal goals? _____

     _____

     _____

   B. What is your desired lifestyle? _____

     _____

     _____

   C. What characteristics associated with your career choice will help you in achieving the lifestyle you described above?

     1. _____

     2. _____

   D. Is your career choice consistent with your personal goals? In what way?

     _____

     _____

     _____

II. Your Interests and Capabilities

   A. Does your career choice require you to use skills or abilities related to your interests? Explain.

     _____

     _____

     _____

   B. Does your career choice require that you possess specific capabilities? List those skills, behaviors, attitudes, or knowledge areas required by your career.

     _____

     _____

     _____

III. Job Characteristics to Consider about Your Tentative Career Choice

   _____

(position desired)

   A. What special training or qualifications are required to enter your chosen career field?

     1. _____

     2. _____

     3. _____

continued

B. What are the general duties or the nature of the work associated with your career choice?

_____
_____
_____

C. Where would you go to get the training required to enter your chosen field?

_____
_____

D. What are the specifics of the training required to enter the career of your choice?
   1. How long will it take? _____
   2. Are there places where you can get financial assistance? ___
   3. Where can you go for help? _____
   4. Will you need to make a personal investment (capital investment, equipment, tools) to enter your chosen field? _____
   5. What will this equipment cost if you purchase it today? ____

E. Are there possibilities for advancement in your career area?
   1. What position could you advance to eventually? _____
      _____
   2. What training or skills do you need to advance in your area?
      _____
      _____
   3. How many months or years of experience will you need in your career area in order to advance to the position you desire?
      _____

F. What are the working environment and conditions associated with your career choice?
   1. Indoors _____   4. Outdoors _____
   2. Hours _____   5. Shift work _____
   3. Hazards _____

G. Are there fringe benefits associated with your career? _____
   _____
   1. Do firms or businesses that hire employees in your area offer these?
      a. Health insurance   Yes____ No____
      b. Life insurance   Yes____ No____

continued

    c. Sick leave   Yes_____ No_____

    d. Vacation time   Yes_____ No_____

2. Are there retirement plans, pension plans, profit-sharing plans, stock options, or savings plans associated with those industries that employ workers in your career choice area?

_____

_____

H. What about wages associated with your career choice?

   1. Hourly wages   Yes_____ No_____

   2. Piece or quantity production wages   Yes_____ No_____

   3. Commissions   Yes_____ No_____

   4. Monthly salary   Yes_____ No_____

   5. Yearly salary   Yes_____ No_____

   6. Docked if you miss work   Yes_____ No_____

IV. Will you be able to get a job in your career area of interest?

A. What is the expected demand for workers employed in this field?

_____

_____

B. Where (geographic location) are large numbers of workers in your career area of interest employed?

_____

Are there possibilities in major cities? _____

_____

Are there possibilities in small towns? _____

_____

C. Does one part of your state need more workers with the skills related to your future career than others? If so, where?

_____

V. Other Jobs You Could Qualify for with the Same Skills

A. List at least three other positions you would qualify for if you possessed all of the skills needed and related to your career choice.

   1. _____

   2. _____

   3. _____

continued

B. List two jobs you could do while you wait for openings related to your career area

1. _____
2. _____

VI. Where and How You Will Seek Information Regarding Openings

A. _____

B. _____

C. _____

D. _____

VII. Ways to Prepare Now?

A. Experience you can obtain:
1. _____
2. _____

B. Courses you can take in school:
1. _____
2. _____
3. _____

VIII. Resources for Additional Information

_____
_____
_____
_____

What will you need to develop, improve, and update your career plan? The following form has some information you should have current and readily available for possible job interviews.

My Personal History

Name _____

Address _____ City _____ Zip _____

Phone _____

Social Security No. _____ VA No. _____

Date of Birth (month, day, year) _____

Marital Status   Single _____   Divorced _____

                 Separated _____   Widowed _____

                 Other _____   How long? _____

Number of children _____   Ages _____

Ethnic background _____

Education History

1. What was the highest grade you completed in school?
   High school graduate? _____ Year _____
   College graduate? _____ Year _____
   Semester completed, if you did not graduate _____
   Technical school graduate? _____ Year _____
   Other (specify) _____

2. What was your major course of study? _____
   Degree (specify field) _____ _____

3. Do you hold any certificates or licenses? Yes _____ No _____
   Certificate (specify) _____
   License (specify) _____

Volunteer History

1. Have you ever done volunteer work? Yes _____ No _____

2. If so, what kind?
   Church _____ School _____ Hospital _____
   Community organizations _____ City, county, or state agencies _____
   Other _____
   Please list:

Date	Affiliation	Duties/Responsibilities	Length of Service

continued

Health Screening

1. How would you describe the status of your general physical health?
   Excellent _____ Good _____ Fair _____ Poor _____

2. Are you bothered by any chronic condition? Yes _____ No _____
   If yes, explain _____
   _____

3. When was the last time you had a complete physical examination?
   Month _____ Year _____

4. Do you have a regular source of health care at this time?
   Yes _____ No _____
   If yes, what source? _____

5. Do you have limitations imposed by a disability? Yes _____
   No _____
   If yes, explain _____
   _____
   Are you regularly taking medication? Yes _____ No _____

6. Were you ever referred to your State Vocational Rehabilitation
   Program?
   Yes _____ No _____
   Receiving AFDC (Aid to Families with Dependent Children) _____
   Welfare _____ Social Security Insurance _____
   Ex-offender _____ Other assistance _____

Use of Resources

1. Have you gone to a Private Industry Council, JTPA (Job Training
   Partnership Act) office for certification?
   Yes _____ No _____

2. Have you gone to a public employment office? Yes _____ No _____
   If yes, explain _____
   _____

3. Have you gone to a private employment agency? Yes _____ No _____
   If yes, explain _____
   _____

4. Other (specify) _____
   _____
   _____

continued

5. Have you investigated whether you are eligible for any of the following types of assistance?

Alimony _____   Social Security _____
VA benefits _____   Pension/retirement benefits _____
Unemployment insurance _____   Disability payments _____
Welfare—Aid to Families with   General assistance _____
Dependent Children _____   Medical _____
Food stamps _____   Other (specify) _____

Assessment of Financial Resources

1. What financial resources do you have available to you?

Income _____   Insurance benefits _____
Savings _____   Disability benefits _____
Social Security _____   VA benefits _____
Other (explain) _____

_____

2. How have you met your living expenses and financial obligations during the past three months?

_____

_____

_____

3. How do you plan to meet your living expenses and financial obligations during the next three to six months?

_____

_____

Personal Profile

1. How do you spend your spare time? Please list hobbies, activities, and so on.

_____

_____

2. What are your reasons for wanting to become involved in a new career? Please check all areas that represent your situation.

_____ a. Explore new directions for my life
_____ b. Meet people with similar problems/goals
_____ c. Receive intellectual stimulation
_____ d. Develop self-confidence
_____ e. Upgrade present skills
_____ f. Develop new skills
_____ g. Other (specify) _____

_____

continued

3. What problems do you face? Check all that apply.
_____ a.   Lack of transportation
_____ b.   Other home responsibilities (care of aged relative, children, and so on)
_____ c.   Lack of personal direction
_____ d.   Language barriers
_____ e.   Educational limitations
_____ f.   Family attitudes toward building a new life
_____ g.   Lack of funds for study or other expenses
_____ h.   Other (specify) _____

Work Values Profile

1. Indicate which factors are important influences toward your satisfaction with a job, using a scale of 1 through 3:

1 - very important
2 - a key consideration
3 - not important

_____ a.   Earning a large salary
_____ b.   Satisfying my family/friends with my career choice
_____ c.   Personal satisfaction with my work
_____ d.   Prestige, "high status"
_____ e.   Intellectual stimulation
_____ f.   Creative flexibility
_____ g.   Job security
_____ h.   Flexible schedule
_____ i.   Helping others
_____ j.   High degree of autonomy
_____ k.   Exciting environment
_____ l.   Challenging work, but without pressure
_____ m. Working by myself
_____ n.   Working as part of a team
_____ o.   Supervising others
_____ p.   Being my own boss

2. Which three of the items listed are most important to you in terms of what you want out of your new job?
_____
_____
_____

continued

Action Plan

1. What are your present goals? Please be specific and identify at least two:
   a. _____
   b. _____

2. What do you think you need to reach your goals? Check all that apply.
   a. Emotional support
      _____ Individual counseling
      _____ Assertiveness training
      _____ Group involvement
   b. _____ Short-term training for skill development
   c. _____ Long-term training for skill development
   d. _____ More education
   e. Recent work experience through
      _____ Trainee placement
      _____ Volunteer placement
   f. Special assistance
      _____ Widowhood counseling
      _____ Marriage-dissolution counseling
      _____ Money management assistance
      _____ Financial assistance
      _____ Other (specify) _____

   g. Job readiness
      _____ Resume writing
      _____ Interviewing techniques
   h. Crisis intervention
      _____ Emergency food
      _____ Shelter
      _____ Legal assistance
   i. Self-employment exploration
      _____ Information
      _____ Financing
   j. Other (specify) _____

Other Considerations

1. Does language pose a barrier to employment or training?
   Yes _____ No _____

continued

2. Will child care pose a problem? Yes _____ No _____
Explain _____
_____
_____

3. Do you have a valid driver's license? Yes _____ No _____

4. Do you have a chauffeur's license? Yes _____ No _____

5. Transportation: Own car _____ Bus _____
                   Family car _____Other _____
                   Friend _____ _____

6. Do you have tools for a specific trade or occupation? Yes _____
No _____
If yes, what type of trade? _____
Do you have any special job skills? _____
What machines have you operated? _____

7. Education and training
Last high school attended _____ City _____
Highest grade completed: 7 8 9 10 11 12
Year of graduation _____

Special courses taken in high school or post-secondary institution:

Shop/ Vocational	Business/ Commercial	Math/Science
_____	_____	_____
_____	_____	_____
_____	_____	_____
_____	_____	_____

Do you have a high school diploma or a GED? Yes _____ No _____
If you have a GED, what is the date of completion? _____
Do you have a copy of your high school transcript or GED scores
attached? Yes _____ No _____

Other training:

Trade School/Business School/Apprenticeship
Name _____ City _____
Type of training _____
Dates attended: from _____ to _____
Date of graduation _____
License or certificate _____

continued

College
Name _____ City _____
Major/minor _____
Credit hours completed _____ Degree _____
Dates attended: from _____ to _____
License or certificate _____

8. Previous employers (list in reverse chronological order)
Employer: _____ Pay rate:
City and state _____
Dates employed: from _____ to _____
Job title _____
Duties/responsibilities _____
_____
_____

Did you receive any specialized training? Yes _____ No _____
If yes, explain _____
_____

Did miss any days on the job? Yes _____ No _____
If yes, explain _____
Why did you leave? _____
Did you like that type of work? Why or why not? _____

Employer: _____ Pay rate:
City and state _____
Dates employed: from _____ to _____
Job title _____
Duties/responsibilities _____
_____
_____

Did you receive any specialized training? Yes _____ No _____
If yes, explain _____
_____

Did miss any days on the job? Yes _____ No _____
If yes, explain _____
Why did you leave? _____
Did you like that type of work? Why or why not? _____

Employer: _____ Pay rate:
City and state _____
Dates employed: from _____ to _____

continued

Job title _____
Duties/responsibilities _____
_____
_____

Did you receive any specialized training? Yes _____ No _____
If yes, explain _____
_____

Did miss any days on the job? Yes _____ No _____
If yes, explain _____
Why did you leave? _____
Did you like that type of work? Why or why not? _____
_____

Employer: _____ Pay rate: _____
City and state _____
Dates employed: from _____ to _____
Job title _____
Duties/responsibilities _____
_____
_____

Did you receive any specialized training? Yes _____ No _____
If yes, explain _____
_____

Did miss any days on the job? Yes _____ No _____
If yes, explain _____
Why did you leave? _____
Did you like that type of work? Why or why not? _____
_____

Testing Options

This chapter is designed to help you determine if you need to take some standardized tests to help you with your career or educational goals now that you have left the military. You may be asking yourself whether or not you should take these tests and wondering what they can do for you and how they can enhance your employment chances.

Benefits of Testing

★★★

Standardized tests measure your behavior, interests, or aptitudes under specific conditions. Your score can be compared with those of thousands of others who took the same test under the same specific conditions; it also can be compared with the score you may receive on the same test at a later date. Thus, the "standardized" in standardized testing means that there are standards or norms of performance expected for specific groups taking the test. These performances are usually classified as high, average, and low. According to *Standardized Tests: A Practical Handbook,* "A standardized test is 'good' if it is useful—if it truly helps us to make better decisions than could have been made without the test results. We say that such a test has 'validity.' "[1] So, if the purpose of a good standardized test is to help you make a decision, you will need a specific set of questions to answer, and you must choose the right test to help you find those answers.

One of the major purposes of testing is to aid in self-understanding. This encompasses helping you determine your personality traits; Are you a thinker or someone who likes to work with their hands? Tests can also help you determine where your strengths, weaknesses, and interests lie. You took numerous tests like this when you first entered the service to help you determine which programs to pursue, for both your own and the military's benefit. The military obviously did research before they decided on what tests to use and to whom to administer them. Now that you are contemplating further testing for your own benefit, you will want to do some delving into what kinds of tests are out there, what they do, who typically uses them, and whether or not they are reputable.

Step One: Research

★★

The first step in your research will be to compile a list of tests currently on the market. According to *Standardized Tests: A Practical Handbook,* there are five excellent sources of information about standardized tests that can be valuable to you as you determine whether certain tests will help you. The sources include the following:

★ *Tests in Print.* This book provides you with a comprehensive list of standardized tests on the market. It contains a subject index so you can search for the specific type of test you are interested in. It should be available at a large public or college library near you, or you can write to

> The Buros Institute of Mental Measurements
> University of Nebraska–Lincoln
> Lincoln, NE 68588-0348

★ *Mental Measurements Yearbooks.* These books are published every two years and provide information on standardized tests that have become available or been revised the past few years. A bonus of this source is that it contains reviews by specialists for most of the tests listed. These objective and authoritative critiques can help you evaluate a test's validity and whether it's right for you. The drawback is that even the most current yearbook may not have accurate information on test prices and forms since the information is only updated every two years. Also, the reviews tend to be quite technical rather than user-friendly. If you can't find a copy at the library near you, contact

> The Buros Institute of Mental Measurements
> University of Nebraska–Lincoln
> Lincoln, NE 68588-0348

★ *Test Critiques.* This set of reference books is published in volumes (the first in 1984), and each volume contains reviews by specialists on the tests that were widely used when that volume was published. These critiques are very user-friendly, and the reviews aren't as technical as those in *Mental Measurements Yearbooks.* If you can't find a copy at the library near you, contact

> PRO-ED
> 8700 Shoal Creek Boulevard
> Austin, TX 78758-6897

★ *Test Publishing.* Good sources to contact are the publishers of the tests themselves because they can offer the most up-to-date information and can refer you to specific tests that will meet your needs. A list of major test publishers is provided at the end of this chapter. Be aware, however, that they will promote their own tests when given the opportunity. They are businesses that need to stay in business!

★ *Users.* You may also want to talk to individuals who have worked with or used the tests that you are considering. Some sources you may wish to contact include a local school, a guidance counselor, a career planning office or job assistance center at a nearby college or university, or a private educational consulting organization.

Once you've used the sources listed here, chosen some tests that apply to your needs, and written to the addresses listed to order some sample tests, you are ready to move on to step three. If you still aren't exactly sure which test is right for you, go to step two, which offers a list of test suggestions.

Step Two: Test Suggestions
★★

Here's a list of tests that you might be interested in as well as where to obtain more information on them.

General Aptitude Test Battery

The General Aptitude Test Battery (GATB) is a nine-score test distributed by the U.S. Employment Service. The total testing time is only about three hours, and the program includes free testing, counseling, and job-referral services. The nine career aptitude test scores are as follows:

1. G = general ability

2. S = spatial ability

3. K = motor coordination

4. V = verbal ability

5. P = form perception

6. F = finger dexterity

7. N = numerical ability

8. Q = clerical perception

9. M = manual dexterity

State employment agencies use a combination of the nine test scores to locate the best candidates for available jobs and to help labor unions locate the best candidates for apprenticeship programs they support.

You can get more information about this program and register for this battery of tests by contacting your local State Employment Services Office, which is listed in the yellow pages of your local phone directory.

ACT–Career Planning Program

American College Testing (ACT) offers a Career Planning Program (CPP) geared for high school and post-high school students to help them evaluate their interests and experience in the following areas:

★ Reading skills

★ Language usage

★ Numerical skills

★ Mechanical reasoning

★ Clerical speed accuracy

★ Space relations

This test may help you assess your strengths and weaknesses in these areas. For more information about this test, contact the ACT Career Services Area.

More tests options are listed later in the chapter. If you still aren't sold on the idea of more testing, maybe you should consider what tests you've already taken and how you can use them now that you are no longer in the military.

Step Three: Review of Previous Tests
★★★

Okay, now you've done some research about standardized testing, and you're getting a better idea of the purpose they serve. Since you're trying to decide if testing is to your benefit, you need to recognize all the testing you've already done and determine exactly what it is you're looking for in more tests. The military has already given you numerous tests to help you determine your strengths, weaknesses, and interests. It may be a good idea to go back over the tests you've already taken, understand what their purpose was, examine your results, and think about how those scores apply to you now that you are pursuing a civilian career.

Armed Services Vocational Aptitude Battery

You're probably pretty familiar with this test, which is distributed by the U.S. Military Entrance Processing Command. The Armed Services Vocational Aptitude Battery (ASVAB) is the primary testing instrument used for military selection and classification by all the services. A nationally normed multiaptitude test, ASVAB is also offered to students in high school grades 10-12, as well as post-secondary school, and is administered to about one million students each year. The ASVAB program includes the following support materials free of charge. You may want to obtain another copy of each.

★ *ASVAB 18/19 Counselor Manual.* This manual is written to support the counselor in administering and using the ASVAB Career Exploration Program. However, since it covers such topics as techniques for administering the ASVAB 18/19 tests, ways of interpreting test results, suggestions on how to use the student workbook and perform a variety of career development activities, it may also be valuable to you.

★ *Exploring Careers: The ASVAB Workbook.* This is an interactive workbook that helps you interpret your ASVAB scores and understand your values, skills, interests, and educational goals. You can also discover how they may be applied in occupations of interest. This workbook is available to everyone who takes the ASVAB.

The manual and workbook can help you interpret what your test results mean today. It would also be good practice for you to complete the career development activities again, especially since you are making a career change.

The ASVAB offers ten career aptitude tests which include the following:

★ General science (GS)

★ Coding speed (CS)

★ Arithmetic reasoning (AR)

★ Auto and shop information (AS)

★ Work knowledge (WK)

★ Mathematics knowledge (MK)

★ Paragraph comprehension (PC)

★ Mechanical comprehension (MC)

★ Numerical operations (NO)

★ Electronics information (EI)

You are given composite scores, which are taken from the ten basic test scores and follow this format:

1. Verbal ability = GS + WK + PC

2. Math ability = AR + MK

3. Academic ability = WK + PC + AR

4. Mechanical/crafts = AR + AS + MC + EI

5. Electrical/electronic = WK + AR + MK + EI

6. Business/clerical = WK + PC + MK + CS

7. Health/social technology = WK + PC + AR + MC

These scores are given to you along with a workbook that focuses on civilian careers and *A Military Career Guide* which provides information on more than 200 military occupations. If you don't have a copy, be sure to request another.

The ASVAB is used in two ways. First, each branch of the armed forces uses it as a selection tool for enlistment purposes and as a classification tool for placement in training programs. Second, it can be used by high school students for both civilian and military career exploration. For this purpose, the Department of Defense has incorporated ASVAB test scores into a more comprehensive career development program (the ASVAB Career Exploration Program). In addition to the ASVAB, the program gives students the opportunity to identify and use Holland interest codes, education, and work values in a process that links personal characteristics to occupational characteristics.

The ASVAB is a vocational aptitude test, meaning it focuses on skills an individual needs in a professional workplace. Fields include sales, office, factory, and construction work. The difference between this type of test and the kind of aptitude test you were given in elementary or middle school is that it covers nonacademic skills, like clerical speed and accuracy. These kinds of tests can identify skills in people that are not readily evident in their academic work. Development and technical information about the program can be obtained from

DoD Testing Center
Defense Manpower Data Center
99 Pacific Street, Suite 155A
Monterey, CA 93940

Step Four: Career Interest Measures
★★

Career interest measures are designed to help you answer questions about your vocational future. If you are applying to college and aren't sure whether to look for a strong business department because you think you might like business or a liberal arts program where you can take a wider range of classes, these tests can help you make your choice. They help you identify your preferences; by combining these preferences with other weighing information, you can decide on and plan your particular educational and/or career future. Not only will they open your eyes to some interests and strengths you may not have known you had, but they will also show you some career options you may never have considered. These measures often play a big part in a complete career planning program and are actively used by many job assistance centers, career planning offices, and employment service agencies.

There are drawbacks to interest measures, however. One is that it is possible, consciously or subsconsciously, to make your results come out the way you want them to. That is the main reason these scores are not used alone, but are compiled with other information. By taking all factors into account, you can make sure you are getting accurate results. Another drawback is that many of the tests are gender biased. You will want to choose a test that uses gender-neutral terminology throughout, so as to obtain more objective test results.

Where can you locate more information on interest measurements? Try the following:

★ The **Association for Interest Measurement (AIM)** conducts research on the popularity of interest measures and collates research reports on them. You can receive copies of these reports by contacting

> Association for Interest Measurements
> 949 Peregrine Drive
> Palatine, IL 60067

★ The **Committee to Screen Career Guidance Instruments (CSCGI)** also publishes reports on popular interest measures and inventories. For information on obtaining copies of these reports, contact

Association for Measurements and Evaluation in Counseling and Development
C/O AACD
5999 Stevenson Avenue
Alexandria, VA 22304

The authors of *Standardized Tests: A Practical Handbook* recommend the following interest measures based on the AIM research studies and the CSCGI reports.

★ **Self-Directed Search.** This interest inventory is distributed by Psychological Assessment Resources and can be purchased without going through a counselor. This is a great way to get career counseling if you don't have direct access to professional services. The test is self-scored, and your scores are made up of a three-letter code. You then go to the occupations booklet that is provided and find the occupations that correspond to your code. This allows you to browse through some career possibilities that your interests and abilities seem best suited for. The codes also correspond with college majors listed in another booklet if you are considering furthering your education. For more information on the Self-Directed Search contact

> Psychological Assessment Resources
> P.O. Box 998
> Odessa, FL 33556

★ **Career Occupational Preference System.** This interest inventory is distributed by EdITS and contains more than 150 job *activities* instead of job *titles*. Each activity lists the kind of educational background usually associated with that profession. Some are listed as "professional," indicating that four or more years of college is required; those listed as "skilled" do not require a degree. For more information about the Career Occupational Preference System, contact

EdITS
P.O. Box 7234
San Diego, CA 92167

★ **Career Decision-Making System.** This interest inventory is distributed by the American Guidance Service, which publishes forms in English, Spanish, and French. The results are converted into six scores and, using the information provided, are organized into career choices that are described in a table of 18 job groups. Information is provided about certain jobs with lists of the educational norms and sources where further information may be obtained. For more information about the Career Decision-Making System, contact

American Guidance Service
Publishers Building
Circle Pines, MN 55014

★ **Kuder Occupational Interest Survey.** This interest inventory is distributed by CTB/SRA and is different from other inventories in that it compares your interests with those of individuals who are established in their careers. Its main purpose is to help you make specific educational and occupational decisions. By locating individuals who share your interests, you can see what it is they are doing and what is required of someone in that profession. The results let you know if you scored high, average, or low compared to other KOIS test-takers. You can also find out how your interests relate to a college major. For more information on the Kuder Occupational Interest Survey, contact

CTB/SRA
2500 Garden Road
Monterey, CA 93940

★ **Strong Interest Inventory.** This interest inventory is distributed by Consulting Psychologists Press, was formerly known as the Strong Vocational Interest Blank and is now known as the Strong-Campbell Interest Inventory (SCH). This test contains more than 300 interest items; you mark each item as like, indifferent, or dislike. This test is popular with many job assistance centers and career planning offices. For more information on the Strong Interest Inventory, contact

> Consulting Psychologists Press
> 3803 East Bayshore Drive
> Palo Alto, CA 94306

★ **Career Assessment Inventory.** This interest inventory is distributed by National Computer Systems and is very similar to the Strong Interest Inventory, except that it focuses more on occupations that do not require a college education. The test consists of more than 350 interest items grouped into three categories: activities, school subjects, and occupations. In addition to your regular results, you will receive a list of more than 100 specific career scores. For more information on the Career Assessment Inventory, contact

> National Computer Systems
> P.O. Box 1416
> Minneapolis, MN 55440

Department of Labor

The Department of Labor is also a good resource. It offers free testing and provides a complete career planning program that includes testing, counseling, workshops, seminars, and databases of jobs and apprenticeships available in your area.

The Department of Labor has developed the Aptitude-Interest Measure, also known as AIM (not to be confused with the Association for Interest Measurement discussed earlier). It is made up of the following two inventories:

1. **General Aptitude Test Battery.** The GATB, which was described earlier, measures your abilities as applied to particular jobs and activities. The results let you know how your abilities match those of individuals working in 66 different employment fields.

2. **Interest Inventory.** The Interest Inventory was developed to measure your likes or dislikes for particular job requirements. The results indicate the strength of your preferences in 12 broad interest areas.

The results from these two tests help you understand your career preferences by helping you assess your interests. They should be used as a guide for further research into the many career paths at hand. You also need to take previous job experience, educational background, training, and job market trends into account when contemplating careers.

A Caution

★★

Now that you have done your research, determined your needs, and discovered what's available in the test market, you need to be aware that there are hawks out there who want to sell you their tests simply because standardized testing can be a very lucrative business. There are just as many bad tests as there are good ones. Make sure you know what it is you are trying to accomplish with testing, and don't let anyone tell you that you have to have more testing to market yourself in today's job world. You had plenty of testing in the service and have received some of the best job training and experience there is. Only pursue further testing if you think it will serve you. If you think more testing will help you make career decisions where you are confused, by all means pursue it, but make sure to do your research and find out which tests are best suited for your needs. Use the list of publishers in the next section in your research.

There are plenty of free tests out there, so use them. During your transition, you'll need to spend your money on more important things than a battery of expensive tests!

Index of Major Test Publishers

American College Testing (ACT)
P.O. Box 168
Iowa City, IA 52243-0168

American Guidance Service (AGS)
Publishers Building
Circle Pines, MN 55014

Consulting Psychologists Press
3803 East Bayshore Drive
Palo Alto, CA 94306

CTB/McGraw-Hill
2500 Garden Road
Monterey, CA 93940

EdITS
P.O. Box 7234
San Diego, CA 92167

Educational Testing Service
Rosedale Road
Princeton, NJ 08541-6736

IPAT
P.O. Box 188
Champaign, IL 61825-0188

National Computer Systems (NCS)
P.O. Box 1416
Minneapolis, MN 55440

PRO-ED
8700 Shoal Creek Boulevard
Austin, TX 78758-6897

Psychological Assessment Resources
P.O. Box 998
Odessa, FL 33556

Psychological Corporation
555 Academic Court
San Antonio, TX 78204

Riverside Publishing Company
8420 Bryn Mawr Avenue
Chicago, IL 60631

Scholastic Testing Service (STS)
P.O. Box 1056
Bensenville, IL 60106-8056

Western Psychological Services
12031 Wilshire Boulevard
Los Angeles, CA 90025

For Further Reading

Buros, O. K. "Fifty Years in Testing: Some Reminiscences, Criticisms and Suggestions." *The Educational Research,* July-August 1977; 9–15.

Cronbach, L. J. *Essentials of Psychological Testing,* 5th ed. (New York: Harper & Row, 1990).

Walsh, W. B., and Betz, N. E. *Tests and Assessment.* (Englewood Cliffs, NJ: Prentice-Hall, 1985).

References

1. Bauernfeind, R. H., Read, R. W., and Wichwire, P. N. *Standardized Tests: A Practical Handbook.* (IL: VCB Books, 1991).

The College Question

How could eating right enhance your chances? How could exercising enhance your chances? How could reading more enhance your chances? Be serious! Granted, college is not right for everyone, and, for many occupations, it is not even necessary. Many times proprietary and trade schools, union-sanctioned training, and/or two-year nondegree colleges are all that is needed to ensure job security, good pay, and excellent benefits. Examples of this are found in the construction business (electricians, masons, plumbers, heavy equipment operators, carpenters, and so on).

But, let's discuss what 60 percent of the population go after—and that is either a two- or a four-year degree. We will also discuss master's degrees and beyond. There is absolutely no question that the more college education you have, the more money you make. In fact, where you go to college affects your income as much as the degree you earn does!

The Facts
★★

Given that you are reading this chapter to find out the "whats" and "where-fores" about going to college, let's start with a few interesting tidbits:

★ Projected total full-time enrollment in two- and four-year colleges for 1994 was 13,200,000.

★ The greatest increase in the college-bound market is the number of nontraditional students.

★ Family and student earnings, savings, and sale of assets are the primary financial resources used to pay for college. This amounts to more than $53 billion annually, or 68.8% of the total bill!

★ More than 50% of college students polled indicated they received a "bum steer" during their college selection process.

★ More than 28% of all qualified students don't even apply to college because they believe they can't afford it *and* less than 20% of these same students accurately estimate the cost of college.

★ Thirty-two percent of all college students do not return for their sophomore year; only 47% of all college students complete their degree requirements.

College Tips for Military Personnel
★★

The following tips are designed to assist you in the college planning process. Everything—from determining how much you can afford to spend to making your final college selection decision—is included. The more information you have regarding this huge financial and personal commitment, the more comfortable you will be in making your final selection.

Finances

Determine how much you will need to spend.

★ Student-need analysis programs can be found in local banks, colleges, military transition centers, many high school guidance offices, and career centers.

★ If you are not quite ready to enter the college market now, use a 7-percent yearly inflation factor to calculate future costs.

College Financial Planning

Budget now for estimated monthly college payments.

★ Many banks not only have excellent low-interest college loans, they also provide home-equity capitalization.

★ Many colleges also offer low-interest monthly payment plans.

★ There are many loans in the marketplace, but as a veteran you will have access to some unique ones. First, there is the SLS loan, which is designed for independent students. Second, there are the federally subsidized loans. Those are the ones that you want; you don't pay interest or principal until nine months after you terminate your education. Finally, many divisions and military units have unique awards and grants for those who have served. Contact your local VFW, American Legion, or Veteran's Affairs office for more information.

★ Use any GI Bill money you have accumulated while in the service immediately, to reduce your asset base and increase your grant and loan eligibility.

Personal Financial Planning

Given personal and college expenses, you will need to adjust your family budget so investments, expenses, and retirement needs are still met.

★ Once you have determined your college spending plan, consult a financial planner for solid advice about other financial issues that may arise.

★ Many banks and financial firms have qualified nonproduct-oriented planners who are only concerned with offering the best advice possible.

College Admissions Tests

Register for appropriate admissions tests, including the SAT, ACT, ACH, and graduate school placement exams. Because you are a nontraditional student, the college may waive the exam requirement.

★ Most colleges require either the SAT or ACT. If you have not taken any of the required exams and the college is requesting that you do so, refer to the next tip on test preparation.

★ Many colleges also require achievement tests. You can study for these exams, and test prep centers are a good place to start.

Test Preparation Courses

Explore college admissions test preparation courses.

★ These courses are available through local high schools, colleges, or private companies. Kaplan and Princeton Review centers are the most widely accepted programs.

★ Studies show that students who participate in such courses tend to improve their test scores.

Academic Review and Interpretation

Evaluate academic patterns on all of your transcripts.

★ Determine academic strengths and weaknesses against specific college admissions requirements.

★ Tailor any military or night courses you may take to meet the admissions requirements at prospective colleges.

Extracurricular Review

Assess school, military, civic, and work-related activities in developing a personal profile.

★ Involvement in extracurricular activities plays an important role in the college admissions process, but don't try to show off for the college admissions counselor.

★ Commitment to one particular activity, club, or group may serve as a "hook" for the more competitive colleges. Your military experience will serve you well.

Interest and Aptitude Testing

Use the results of interest and aptitude tests to define areas of college study.

★ Explore occupations and careers related to strengths in your personal and academic profile. Your ASVAB result is a wonderful way to start.

★ Test results often help to identify specific jobs within career clusters. By now, you should have some ideas as to where you want to start.

Self-Assessment

Assess academic, social, and personal performance in determining future plans and goals.

★ Set realistic goals based on past performance. Don't underassess your strengths or weaknesses.

★ An honest self-evaluation is invaluable in the college planning process.

College Majors and Occupations

Look at colleges with broad programs of study that interest you. Remember: No job has to be forever. Examine both short- and long-term interests and job availability.

★ Limiting yourself to one major may cause you to overlook colleges that are worthy of consideration.

★ Thoroughly investigate the depth of programs at your colleges of interest.

Target Colleges

Develop a realistic list of colleges based on your personal parameters.

★ Consider your financial status, academic records, interest and aptitude test results, geographical preferences, special talents or disabilities, and other important factors.

★ Your list should include colleges with varying admission standards.

Support Services

Consider the availability of support services at each college.

★ Tutoring, learning disability programs, remedial courses, career planning, and counseling are all available at the college level.

★ Determine early on the need for such services and personally interview a representative from the service in question.

Campus Activities

Consider the nonacademic activities offered at each college.

★ An accurate evaluation of your athletic performance in high school and the military can help you find an appropriate match at the college level.

★ Seek out the activities that most interest you at various colleges.

Campus Visits and Interviews

Arrange and prepare for campus visits and interviews.

★ Begin visiting college campuses as soon as possible. If you are still in the service, request an appointment time that is convenient for you.

★ Set up appointments with admissions offices well in advance for college interviews and tours. Don't forget to talk to the college planning and placement office as well; staff can give you accurate feedback as to how their graduates are doing.

Scholarships

Identify local, national, merit, college-allocated, need, and nonneed-based awards.

★ Investigate your eligibility for local, national, and college-related scholarships.

★ Scholarships and grants are available on a ''need'' and ''no-need'' basis, depending on the college or administering agency.

Additional Colleges

Reevaluate your original list of colleges based on your campus visits and the information you obtained.

★ On the basis of your impressions and interviews, consider adding or eliminating colleges to or from the list.

★ The availability of monies at specific colleges may influence your final list of possibilities.

Summer Programs and Jobs

Participate in summer programs that will enhance the personal profile. If you have the time and resources between your military service and your college entrance date, consider internships or college summer programs.

★ Numerous programs are available, from summer college courses to college internship positions.

★ Summer employment offers an excellent opportunity to explore various career interests.

Applications

Complete college applications well ahead of the deadlines.

★ An organized, well-written application will ensure the best opportunity for admission.

★ Many colleges require essays that demand a lot of time and effort. Give yourself plenty of time to complete these sections.

Financial Aid

Fill out the appropriate college financial aid forms as soon as possible.

★ Check on deadlines so you won't miss out on possible awards, grants, and/or loans.

★ Doublecheck your answers to questions; inaccurate or incomplete information will delay or prevent the processing of your forms.

Decision

Select the college that best meets your personal, family, and financial needs.

★ Together with your family, reevaluate your priorities given the opportunities that have become available.

★ Careful evaluation of financial aid packages may be an important factor in your final decision. This may be negotiable!

Acceptance and Enrollment Forms

Submit your enrollment deposit and other required forms before specified college deadlines.

★ Pay strict attention to instructions on the forms in order to avoid penalties of any kind.

★ An enrollment deposit is often required well in advance.

College Payment Plans

Devise a college payment plan that best suits your financial situation.

★ Once you have made your final college selection, investigate specific payment programs offered by the college.

★ You may be eligible for nongovernment-subsidized interest-only loans. Payment on the principal does not begin until after graduation or termination from college.

Transferring

If you have had previous college experience, you may be able to transfer those credits to your new program. Consult with the college to which you are applying about the eligibility of credits. Make sure you have transcripts available. Transfer only when you have looked at all the options available to you and after you have discussed your acceptable transfer credits with a transfer admissions counselor.

★ Once your transfer has been accepted, be sure to visit the financial aid office to discuss a financial aid package. Timing is important, so start early.

★ Grades are critical. If you do well in courses before transferring, it will increase your transfer options.

Graduate School

Undergraduate grades in your chosen major, as well as your cumulative grade point average, weigh heavily with graduate schools.

★ Taking the correct Graduate Record Examinations at the appropriate time is critical.

★ Many times ''field experience'' is either necessary or recommended before you will be considered by a graduate school.

Remember:

You are in a buyer's market. Colleges will often relax their acceptance standards for nontraditional students. They know you are a "sure bet" to complete your graduation requirements. You are more mature and more sophisticated than your straight-from-high-school counterparts. You will be concerned about achieving academic success at college, but don't worry! Your perseverance will carry you through. One last tip: *Don't be afraid to ask for help!*

Financial Aid

★★

Financial aid is one of the key factors in deciding to go to college and in selecting an appropriate one. Let's briefly look at the three major steps in the financial aid process.

★ Analyzing your financial need. The amount of your need will vary depending on the cost of education at your particular school. The cost of education is the amount required to cover tuition and fees, room and board, books and supplies, transportation, and miscellaneous expenses. Your expected family contribution (EFC) is the amount of your family's—or your—financial resources assumed to be available for college payments. This amount is based on a federal formula and requires completion of the Free Application for Federal Student Aid. The EFC does not vary by the cost of education at a particular college. The cost of education less your EFC equals your financial need.

★ Building a financial aid package. After you have determined your financial need, the college's financial aid office works with you to meet this need by putting together a financial aid package. Your college may require the completion of supplemental aid applications. Financial aid is the total amount you receive from the college or outside sources, including grants, scholarships, work-study and certain government loans such as the Subsidized Federal Stafford. Financial aid often, but not always, meets your needs. Your financial need minus the financial aid you receive equals your total unmet financial need.

★ Computing your actual cost. You need to know how much you are expected to pay toward the cost of your education. Your actual cost for attending a particular college consists of two factors: unmet need (if any) and EFC. Unfortunately, this actual cost is often more than a family is able to pay from its assets and monthly income. You may need a loan to meet this cost.

College Loans

After calculating the actual cost of attending the college of choice, you may find you need a loan. Through your personal relationship with various lenders, credit unions, banks, or your VA office, you will be able to access most or all of the loans described in the following subsections.

Government Loans

Although not all government loans are based on financial need, loan applicants must complete the Free Applicant for Federal Student Aid (FAFSA). Federal guidelines defining the amount that may be borrowed and the requirements for loan applications change frequently. A college financial aid officer can answer your questions about completing financial aid forms and provide detailed information about government loans.

Federal Stafford Loan–Subsidized. The Subsidized Stafford is a need-based loan for undergraduate students and may be authorized as part of your college's financial package. You must apply for the loan through an approved lender. Freshmen may borrow up to $2,625 per year; sophomores may borrow a maximum of $3,500 per year. Other undergraduates may borrow up to $8,500 per year. No undergraduate student can borrow more than $23,000 for all four years. The maximum you may borrow for both undergraduate and graduate studies is $65,000. An origination fee of 5% and an insurance fee of up to 3% will be deducted from the proceeds of each Stafford loan. Loan repayment is deferred until six months after graduation or until the student is no longer enrolled. When repayment begins, the interest rate is variable and cannot exceed 9%.

Federal Stafford Loan–Unsubsidized. This new loan allows those who aren't financially needy to borrow under the Stafford program. This loan can also be used if you aren't awarded the maximum amount under the Subsidized Stafford. The program has the same low interest rate and borrowing limits as the Subsidized Stafford; however, the student must pay interest while enrolled. Like the Subsidized Stafford, repayment of the principal begins six months after graduation. An origination/insurance fee of 6.5% is deducted from the proceeds of each Unsubsidized Stafford loan.

Federal Parent Loans for Undergraduate Students. This loan may be applicable if either your parents are contributing to your transition to college or you are financing a child's education. Borrowers of this loan are not required to show financial need, and there are no annual or total loan limits. Parents may borrow up to the total cost of education less any financial aid received. The interest rate is guaranteed not to exceed 10%. An origination fee of 5% and an insurance fee of up to 3% are deducted from the proceeds of each loan. Repayment of principal and interest begins after the student is enrolled.

Federal Supplemental Loans for Students.   This is a loan for independent undergraduate, graduate, and professional school students who do not receive parental financial support. Generally, students qualifying for this program are 24 years of age or older. Students are not required to show financial need. Maximum amounts vary from $4,000 in the freshman and sophomore years to $5,000 in the junior and senior years to $10,000 per year for graduate studies. Undergraduates may borrow a total of $23,000. The maximum debt for combined undergraduate and graduate studies is $73,000. An origination fee of 5% and an insurance fee of up to 3% are deducted from the proceeds of each loan. The interest rate is variable and is guaranteed not to exceed 11%. Repayment of the principal is deferred as long as the student is enrolled at least half time; however, the student is required to pay interest while enrolled.

Private Loans

With the potential for income tax deduction (your tax advisor will know the details) or a cash rebate, a private loan may be your most convenient and attractive option. You don't have to prove financial need and aren't required to complete a needs analysis form.

Home Equity Loans

Because its interest may be tax deductible, a home equity loan could be your family's lowest cost loan. Interest rates on home equity loans may be either fixed or variable. The types of loans range from fully amortizing loans to home equity lines of credit. The credit line also includes an option for interest-only payments while you are enrolled in college.

Philanthropic Loans

A wellspring of below-market or low-cost loans is the philanthropic lending sector. These private lenders (often the same people who dispense scholarships) may not require a need analysis test. Here are examples of organizations and civic-minded lending institutions that could help in your quest for thrifty loans.

Pictett and Hatcher Educational Fund, Inc.
P.O. Box 8169
Columbus, GA 31908

- Funds available to students who live in and attend colleges in the southeastern United States.
- Money goes to students in colleges that offer broad liberal arts education other than preparation for careers in law, medicine, or the ministry.
- Maximum loan is $3,000 per academic year, maximum total is $12,000.

The Scholarship Foundation of St. Louis
8215 Clayton Road
St. Louis, MO 63117

- Applicants must be residents of the St. Louis area and high school graduates with financial need.
- Loans are for undergraduate, graduate, and vocational-technical schools.
- Maximum loan award is $3,000 a year; maximum total is $15,000.

Myers-MacEachern Student Loans
Foundation of Record Education of AHIMA
Suite 1400
919 N. Michigan Avenue
Chicago, IL 60611

- Students must be enrolled full-time in health information technology or an administration program in final year of study.
- Maximum loan for technology is $2,000; administration is $3,000.

J.C. Stewart Memorial Trust
7718 Finns Lane
Lanham, MD 20706

- Candidates must be Maryland residents attending an accredited institution.
- Interest only payable until six months after leaving school. Repayment is made in monthly installments.
- Maximum loan award is $2,500 per academic year.

Company-Sponsored Loans

If you take a job straight out of the military, and then decide you'd like more education, it's not too late and there may be resources available to you. Large corporations sometimes make below-market-rate college loans available for employees' children. If the company has a savings plan, you may be able to borrow from your account in it.

For instance, many U.S. Chamber of Commerce member companies sponsor CONSERN LOANS FOR EDUCATION, a low interest, long-term loan. For information, ask your company human resources specialist.

Tuition Payment Plans

Tuition plans are offered by banks, colleges, insurance companies, and specialized financial management firms. Two examples of these firms are as follows:

Knight Tuition Payment Plans/College Resource Group
855 Boylston Street
Boston, MA 02116

Tuition Management Systems, Inc.
42 Valley Road
Newport, RI 02840

Scholarships

Millions of dollars in private scholarship funds are awarded to college students each year. However, contrary to popular belief and promotional mailings from scholarship search firms, there are no billions, or even millions, that go unawarded each year and to which you may have access.

While there is a lot of money available from all sources to help all types of people pursuing higher education, in reality, these amounts do not go unawarded. Those promotional claims include large corporate educational funds for their own employees and do not represent money available to the typical college-bound student. Don't believe all the claims you hear about excess scholarship monies. But, there are some proactive things you can do about scholarships and/or grants:

★ Contact your transition office at the military base nearest your new residence. It may have the CASHE scholarship search program on its computers. Also, even though you have been out of school for a while, don't hesitate to contact a high school guidance department to find information on scholarships.

★ Contact colleges to which you are considering applying. Inquire if they have special scholarships, such as academic merit, talent, or athletic funds that are not awarded on a financial need basis.

★ If you are going to use a scholarship search firm, inquire about guarantees and get details.

Choosing a College

★★

Now that you have your finances arranged, your final task is to spend several hours at your local library, transition center, community college admissions office, or high school guidance office over a period of a few days. Ask the person in charge for several guides that describe and compare colleges. Look up the schools on your list and take notes. Most large public schools and some libraries and transition centers have college searches on computer; ACT's Discover and Houghton Mifflin's GIS are two excellent examples. You can expect to find the following information about schools in these guides:

★ **General information.** This includes the geographic location of the college and some idea as to whether the campus is in an urban or rural setting. The accrediting body is mentioned, as are the enrollment figures for undergraduates. A brief description of the libraries, research facilities, and other buildings may also be included.

★ **Student-to-faculty ratio.** These figures tell you how many students there are for each instructor, giving you an idea of how much personal attention you are likely to receive from teachers.

  Some guides will also tell you the percentage of faculty holding doctoral degrees; the higher this percentage, the more prestigious the faculty is likely to be. You need to be aware, however, that the actual teaching may be done by their assistants.

★ **Profile of undergraduates.** A large number of figures could be presented under this heading, such as the percentage of freshman undergraduates, the number of male and female students, minority enrollment, the number of students receiving financial aid, and the number of international students. If being among a certain group of people is important to you, examine these figures closely.

★ **Freshman data.** This section outlines information about the last class that entered the college. It will give you an idea of how many students applied and were accepted. Also included are their average SAT or ACT test scores and their average class rank on graduation from high school. These figures allow you to compare yourself academically to the average freshman at a particular college. You may also get an idea of how competitive the school is likely to be; the higher the marks, the more difficult the academic load.

★ **Expenses.** These figures include tuition, fees, and books. If you plan to live on campus, room and board figures are included. Many guides also give an estimated figure for miscellaneous expenses likely to occur within a one-year period.

★ **Financial aid.** These figures are the most important for many people. Many students drop a college from their list because of the expense involved. As we've discussed, all schools have financial aid offices from which a variety of financial aid packages can be developed. There are basically four types of financial aid: scholarships, loans, grants, and jobs. Applicants usually qualify on the basis of financial need, academic excellence, or athletic achievement. Financial aid packages run from $200 to all expenses for the year.

You must examine the large numbers and types of financial aid devices as soon as possible because many programs require you to file statements concerning your ability to pay your college expenses.

★ **Admissions.** This section will reveal what is required of applicants. The usual requirements include high school transcripts, test scores, teacher recommendations, and any requirements for early admission. Requirements for early admission usually include high grades, high test scores, or outstanding athletic ability. If an interview is required, it will be noted. The deadline for applications is also provided.

★ **Transfer admissions.** Most of the requirements listed for regular admissions will apply, and your present college transcript will be needed.

★ **Special programs.** Many of these programs are remedial in nature: however, any cooperative programs with other colleges are listed here. Any programs unique to the college, such as exchange programs, are also mentioned.

★ **Career services.** This is an important service if you are still unsure of your new career direction.

★ **Housing.** You can learn about any restrictions applied to freshman residents, as well as the availability of on-campus housing.

★ **Student life.** This section includes the college regulations governing student behavior on campus.

★ **Athletics.** Competitive intercollegiate sports programs, as well as any intramural programs, will be mentioned.

★ **Organizations.** Fraternities, sororities, and academic organizations such as honor societies and on-campus groups interested in specific areas of study will be identified here.

★ **Programs of study or majors.** This may be the most important section to you. You can eliminate many schools that do not provide a program of study in which you are interested. The major fields of study that lead to undergraduate degrees will be listed. If your area of interest is not listed, you can eliminate that college from further consideration.

   In some guides, the list seems endless, but the availability of many fields of study gives you greater flexibility should you decide to change majors in a year or two.

★ **Graduates.** Some guides will give you the percentage of freshmen that drop out as well as the percentage that eventually graduate. Some will list the percentage going on for advanced degrees. Pay close attention to this figure if you think you may want to enter graduate school.

★ **Services.** Many colleges offer free services, such as career counseling and remedial instruction.

On the basis of your close examination of each of the sections in the college guides, you can eliminate many colleges from your list. Some will appear too competitive, others lacking in appropriate financial aid, in the wrong geographical location or offering a student environment you find unacceptable. Most importantly, many schools will not offer the programs of study you desire.

Applying to Colleges

At this point, you have considered all the available information in comparative guides and college catalogs. You know what you want from a school and which schools can best provide it. So, which schools should you apply to? If you can be considered a qualified applicant at all the schools on your list and you can meet the financial requirements, you should apply to no more than six colleges (obviously, the top six on your list). Keep in mind that qualified applicants get into their colleges of choice 75 percent of the time. If you have chosen wisely, you're likely to be accepted to most of the schools to which you apply.

   You may be accepted to several schools before you finally decide on one. You should rank the colleges to be certain of your first choice.

Visiting the Campus

On receiving a letter of acceptance you have one more way in which to consider a particular college: Visit it. Spend a day (not on a weekend) walking around the grounds and observing the students, the buildings (especially the library and student center), and the overall atmosphere. Does the environment appear right for you? Are the grounds what you expected?

Talk with some of the students. Are they happy with the education they're getting? What do they like and dislike about the school? See if you can arrange to spend a weekend at the school to get a real sense of what campus life might be like.

Talk to the people in the admissions office and have them arrange for you to sit in on classes in your planned area of study. Ask to visit the science labs, the foreign language labs, and so on while classes are in session so you can see for yourself if the facilities are state-of-the-art.

Waiting to Hear

What if you haven't heard from your top choice before other acceptances come in? Some colleges want a deposit holding your place and give you a limited amount of time to respond.

You have two choices. The first is to write a letter to schools that accepted you and request a later date for your answer. The second is to send the deposit and risk losing it should you be accepted at your first-choice college and decide to go there instead. Most schools have the same deadline date, which should give you enough time to hear from all your choices. Chances are good that you will get a positive response from four of the six schools you apply to and that one of them will be one of your top two choices.

Your Job Search

The key to finding a job is sheer luck and timing, being in the right place at the right time. *The key to landing a job is who you know, not what you know.* Think of your job search as a sales campaign. When planning a sales campaign, the following elements are critical:

★ **Product:** what you're selling; that is, skills, talents, expertise, experience, and potential

★ **Market:** who will buy what you're selling; in this case, potential employers

★ **Strategies:** methods you'll use to reach your customers

★ **Selling tools:** specific "sales" approaches, depending on the customer

★ **Closing techniques:** strategies for closing or finalizing a sale; that is, receiving a job offer

There are many parallels between a sales campaign and a job search. In the job search, you are the product. Before you bring the "product" to market, you need to define not only its features, but also what benefits it (you) would bring to customers or, in this case, employers. In a job search, the "market" refers to all potential employers who could possibly hire you. These represent your target companies, or clients if you're thinking of going into consulting work. There are four ways to reach your customers in a job search: responding to ads, dealing with search consultants or employment agencies, sending targeted mailings, and networking. Once you're identified your customers or target companies, you need to prepare the means by which you will reach your targets. In a job search, "selling tools" are resumés, cover letters, the telephone, and, of course, interviewing. Closing techniques (such as negotiation strategies and handling multiple offers) help to finalize the deal.

The first step in the job search is to define and describe the product, or what you are selling. Why should someone hire you? Take some time to look at yourself and write down the following information:

★ Your skills

★ Your areas of expertise (describe in detail)

★ Your accomplishments (try to list at least 10)

★ Your unique personal characteristics

Next, think about where you want to apply your talents. Your answers to the following questions will help you formulate your "ideal job characteristics."

★ What are your geographical limitations? Preferences?

★ How much are you willing to travel as a part of your job?

★ What distance are you willing to commute to your new job (in terms of minutes, hours, or miles)?

★ What are your salary expectations?

★ What industry do you wish to focus on?

★ What kind of company are you looking for (consider size, growth potential, profitability, product line, and so on)?

★ What type of boss and/or corporate culture do you work best with?

These parameters will prove tremendously helpful once you begin to contact your network and go on interviews. Furthermore, this type of self-awareness will help you to make more effective decisions once you start to receive offers. The "Methods" section of this book goes into more detail about job-search techniques.

Navigating the Job Market

Before you begin to market yourself (look for a job) you need to understand the nature of the job market. People find jobs in one of four ways: (1) responses to classified ads; (2) placements by search firms or employment agencies; (3) direct contact with employers; or (4) personal contacts, or networking. However, not all of these methods are equally effective; their average placement rates are as follows:

Method	*Placement Rate*
Networking	70%
Search firms and employment agencies	15%
Direct contacts	10%
Ad responses	5%

Keep these figures in mind when planning your job search. Don't waste your time solely on passive methods, such as responding to ads and contacting agencies. When you respond to an ad or deal with a "headhunter," your resumé has to be mailed or faxed to a "screener." Because of the sheer number of resumés in circulation, this drastically reduces the chances of your being selected for an interview. As a result, what you get for all your effort is a bunch of rejection letters or no response at all. This avalanche of rejection can lead to a downward spiral of self-confidence (as we discussed in Chapter 2), and the next thing you know, you will say, "I'll never get a job;" "No one will

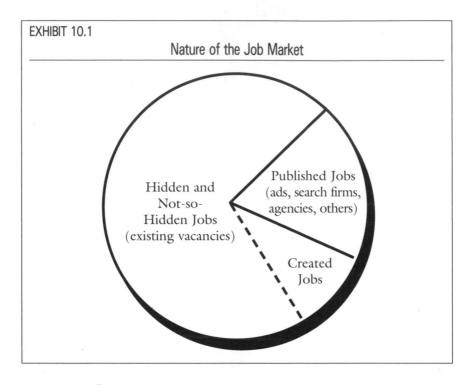

EXHIBIT 10.1

Nature of the Job Market

Hidden and Not-so-Hidden Jobs (existing vacancies)

Published Jobs (ads, search firms, agencies, others)

Created Jobs

ever hire me;" "I'm a worthless human being, a failure." These erroneous, self-limiting beliefs can make you want to give up trying.

An effective job search encompasses all four methods. Here are some guidelines to follow as you plan your search.

First, take a look at the pie chart in Exhibit 10.1. There are two dimensions to the job market. The Formal Job Market is comprised of all the jobs published in newspapers, trade journals, and magazines, as well as the jobs listed with public and private employment agencies and search firms. Because these job opportunities are "published" to the general public, competition for them is extremely intense. For instance, a block ad for a professional position can draw anywhere from 50 to 1,500 responses! Moreover, in order to be considered for these openings, job searchers need to deal with recruiters, human resource professionals, or agency interviewers. These interviewers screen myriad resumés every day. Because of the sheer number of pieces of paper they must scan, being selected for an interview is merely a "numbers game." Moreover, agencies and search firms are paid to find people for jobs. That is, they are hired by companies to search for a particular type of talent or skill. The chances of a search consultant's looking for a candidate exactly matching your background at the time your resumé arrives is extremely low. Therefore, you should not spend a lot of time answering ads or going to employment services.

The bulk of your job-search efforts should be focused on the hidden and not-so-hidden job market. These are jobs which are available, or soon will be, due to turnover caused by retirements, promotions, transfers, terminations, and demotions. Many of these opportunities don't get published, nor are personnel departments aware of what is happening throughout their organizations. The best way to find out about these jobs is through the human information exchange process, also known as networking. In addition, by contacting employers (decision makers) directly, you can learn about hiring needs faster and more accurately than by dealing with personnel or agency interviewers.

Advertisements
★★

Although you shouldn't focus your job-search efforts on responding to ads, you shouldn't ignore them completely. Classified ads are published in newspapers, trade journals, professional society newsletters, magazines, and special-interest publications. They are arranged alphabetically by job title and tend to be very specific in terms of job requirements and qualifications. Although these ads appear in daily newspapers, the best day to scan the classifieds is in the Sunday edition, when the greatest selection appears. When reading the classifieds, use a marker or highlighter to identify the ads that appeal to you. Once you have finished scanning, go back and carefully review each of the ads you highlighted. You will find that some may not be as interesting as you thought, and others will be close to your ideal job.

Bear in mind that there are two types of ads in the classified section: open and blind ads. An open ad reveals the name of the employer and may also list the personnel department contact. Blind ads provide a post office box only, thereby hiding the identity of the employer. This method is used for various reasons: The employer does not want to be bothered with telephone calls or "drop-ins;" the employer wishes to collect resumés prior to terminating the incumbent; the employer wants to remain anonymous because of reputation; or the ad was placed by a search firm or agency in order to "source" resumés. You would do well to ignore blind ads entirely for two reasons: (1) You have no idea where your resume is being forwarded; and (2) You can't follow up your response with a telephone call.

Spend your time wisely and respond to open ads. An effective ad response requires a cover letter and a resumé, both of which are covered in more detail in the "methods" section of this book. Basic points to remember are highlighted here. Keep the cover letter brief and limit it to one page. Here's how to structure your letter.

Paragraph 1 I recently read with interest your ad for _____ and think my skills match your requirements.

Paragraph 2 Qualifications summary (tailor to ad).

Paragraph 3 In terms of salary, my expectations are in the _____ range. I am willing to negotiate depending on the total compensation package. *or* I will be happy to discuss my salary requirements with you during the interview.

Paragraph 4 Closing and how/when to contact you.

Be sure to keep a copy of your letter and the ad to which you responded. Keep a "tickler file" of ad responses to remind you when a follow-up call should be placed (after a week to ten days). Also keep the following general rules in mind:

1. Answer ads for which you are qualified and overqualified.

2. Analyze the ad. Structure your response; the letter should respond to clearly identified needs.

3. Answer ads placed by companies where you have applied before.

4. Watch for companies that place a lot of ads.

5. Watch for ads placed by companies that employ friends.

6. Send impressive cover letters and resumés.

7. Delay responding by five days because the typical response pattern is usually as follows:

Sunday	Ad appears
Monday	15 resumes received
Tuesday	80 resumes received
Wednesday	75 resumes received
Thursday	40 resumes received
Friday	10 resumes received

Dealing with Search Firms and Employment Agencies
★★

The key to dealing with a search consultant or agency interviewer is to remember that these firms specialize in finding people for jobs. They *do not find jobs for people!* Search consultants and agency interviewers will not market you or try to sell you to employers in your area. Rather, they spend their time seeking assignments from client companies (the people who pay their fees) and searching for qualified candidates who fit the employer's needs.

Although the manner in which they operate is similar, search firms and employment agencies differ in terms of the types of jobs they handle.

Search Firms

Search firms operate on either a contingency or retainer basis. Contingency firms are paid by client companies if they actually place a candidate with that company, and the person remains on the job for a specified amount of time, usually spelled out in a contract.

Retainer search firms are paid by client companies to perform certain tasks, regardless of whether a firm places a candidate. These tasks may have to do with screening qualified candidates, performing background checks, or simply finding candidates.

Contingency search firms generally deal with jobs in the $40,000 to $80,000 salary range. Retainer firms usually handle jobs in the $75,000 and higher salary range.

How do you find a search firm? A helpful resource is "The Directory of Executive Recruiters," listed in Chapter 11. You should ask your contacts for suggestions regarding which firm to use. Also, search firms frequently advertise in trade journals and selected professional publications. Make a list of 15 to 25 search firms and send out resumés and cover letters to each firm. It is best to stagger your mailings to improve your chances of the firm's conducting a search for a candidate like you at the time your letter arrives. Follow these guidelines when writing your cover letter:

RE: (Position)

Paragraph 1 Enclosed is my resumé for review against your client assignments.

Paragraph 2 Qualifications summary

Paragraph 3 Compensation requirements (express as a range).

Paragraph 4 Closing and how/when to contact you.

You should keep a record of the firms you have contacted; however, you need not bother to follow up your letter. Search consultants don't take kindly to "pestering" follow-up calls. Most will acknowledge receipt of your paperwork with a postcard, and you can expect at least a cursory telephone interview if the search firm has a possible opportunity for you.

Employment Agencies

Employment or placement agencies operate on a contingency basis; that is, they are paid by client companies only when they place a candidate in a job. Agencies generally handle jobs in the $15,000 to $40,000 salary range. They tend to specialize in a specific field, such as technical, secretarial, or medical.

The yellow pages of your telephone directory are a good source for agencies. Look under "Employment Agencies" or "Personal Recruiters."

Note that search firms and employment agencies operate on an "employer-fee-paid" basis; that is, the client company, not the job applicant, pays the fee. However, some states allow placement agencies to assess fees for obtaining interviews or job placements. You should always ask the placement interviewer: "Are you an employer-fee-paid agency?" Also, do not sign anything unless you have read it carefully. You could be signing a promise to pay a fee simply for the agency's referring you to a job interview.

Direct Contact and Targeted Mailings
★★

Clearly, responding to ads and going to employment agencies are passive, low-yield approaches to getting a job. You will achieve better results if you use the active, high-yield methods, such as direct contact and targeted mailings.

Direct Contact

Make a list of companies within one hour of your new home that appeal to you or appear suitable for employment opportunities. For resources, use the telephone directory yellow pages, Chamber of Commerce literature, and trade and business publications. Also, consider driving through industrial parks for ideas on which companies to add to the list.

Once your list is complete, indicate those companies where you know someone. These are the companies you can approach through networking (see the next section). Prepare a schedule for contacting the remaining companies either through personnel departments or by selected mailings.

One way to find a job is simply to show up on the employer's doorstep. Take a supply of resumés with you and visit the personnel departments of each of the companies on the list. In large companies, the personnel department will frequently give a screening interview to applicants (often called "walk-ins") who show up during a specific window of time, often between 8:00 A.M. and 10:00 A.M. Walk-ins are asked to fill out an employment application and are interviewed by the personnel staff on the spot. In some cases, they may also interview with the hiring manager on the same day. Promising applicants are advised of the company's hiring needs and anticipated time frames for future openings and interviews.

Targeted Mailings

There are two types of targeted mailings: broadcast letters and marketing letters. In a broadcast letter, you literally "shotgun" your availability to employers. This technique is appropriate when you are targeting companies outside your geographic area. A cover letter and copy of your resumé are sent to the personnel or human resources departments of your selected companies. You then wait for a response; no follow-up is required.

A marketing letter is more of a "rifle shot" approach in which you write directly to decision makers at your targeted companies without including your resumé. In addition, the marketing letter approach requires that you follow up the letter with a telephone call in order to assess the hiring manager's needs and/or to arrange a meeting.

Networking
★★

Since most job openings are not normally advertised by companies and organizations, there is a hidden job market. The job openings in this market are known only to people close to the source and news of their availability is passed along to others by word of mouth. To gain access to the hidden job market, you need to go through a systematic process of contacting people.

Networking involves making contacts with everybody you know who may be in a position to tell you of potential job openings or who may know someone else who has such knowledge. This includes relatives, friends, associates and acquaintances from the military, former employers, and fellow church members.

The best way to begin networking is to take a sheet of paper and write down the names of everyone you can think of who fit in the following categories.

★ Friends and relatives

★ People with whom you've served

★ Neighbors/acquaintances

★ Professional associations

★ Former employers

★ Consultants

★ Business owners

★ Common interest associates

★ Club members

★ People you've met while traveling

★ College associates

★ Clergy

★ Salespeople

★ Bankers

★ Lawyers/accountants

★ Doctors/dentists

★ Insurance/real estate agents

★ Civic leaders/politicians

Your Existing Contact Network

Everybody has contacts. Life would be impossible without them. Your existing contact network may not contain decision makers in your career field, but a few carefully selected people will be useful as a starting point on which to build your own career contact network.

Networking does not mean begging for a job. Networking is a process of asking for information, help, guidance, suggestions, counsel, wisdom, advice, feedback, referrals, and support. *Remember: If you're not asking for a job, you won't be rejected!*

Start by contacting those you know best, such as close friends and relatives. This will let you practice your approach and sharpen and refine your technique. Once you have contacted everybody on your list, you will need to move on to individuals you do not know personally, but to whom you have been referred. One way to accomplish this is through the informational interview.

Informational Interviews

An informational interview is often used to gain access to a company for potential job opportunities as well as to learn about opportunities elsewhere. Typically, it is arranged through a phone call or letter with a well-placed person in your chosen field. A request is made to meet with the individual to gain information about your field and the people and organizations in it. It is important to locate an individual whose position will provide you with the right information. In this regard, it is often helpful to use a personal contact's name when you are attempting to arrange an interview.

When writing a letter, always specify a date when you will call to request a meeting. When calling, try to arrange a meeting; if this is not possible, ask your questions on the phone. Do not attempt to secure a position with that individual's firm, but let him or her know you are looking for a job.

When you are able to meet with the person, it is important to take your resumé along and to leave a copy with him or her. Your questions should center around your particular field, new developments in it, who is doing what, and so on. It is appropriate to ask for referrals to other sources of information. Ask for the person's response to your military background and what he or she sees as realistic and possible in your career transition. Make the meeting reasonably short and send a thank-you note afterward.

Although an information interview may seem like a roundabout way of searching for a job, keep in mind that its purpose is not to secure employment, but to gain information about where potential jobs are.

Summary
★★

As you can see, networking is the most effective method of job searching. We discuss ways to find contacts and build a network in Chapter 13. Although it is important, this should not be your only job-search activity. Structure your search plan around all four methods—networking, search firms and employment agencies, direct contacts and targeted mailings, and responses to ads—to make sure you cover all your bases. If you are still in the military, you have the advantage of being able to take more time to prepare for each of these job-hunting techniques.

Researching Your Target Companies

Just as in selling a new product, when you are selling yourself, you must learn all you can about your potential customers in order to market yourself effectively. Before actually going out and "looking" for a job, you should take the time to gather information regarding your market. As we discussed in Chapter 9, you need the following information to develop your job search strategy:

★ What you are "selling," that is, your talent, skills, and abilities

★ The companies or industries that are likely to need or want your skills

★ The level or title of the individual who will actually hire you, that is, the decision maker

★ The locations of the firms that interest you

★ The general salary range for the positions you are seeking

It is important to do your research before you begin making contacts in the marketplace. With this information, you will be knowledgeable regarding industry trends and company reputations and able to demonstrate initiative and preparedness to interviewers and contacts.

What to Research
★★★

As a general rule, you should obtain as much information as possible about your target companies prior to making contact. Use the following outline as a guide to what information is most relevant:

Information about industries
- ★ Historic trends
- ★ Current events
- ★ Noteworthy companies within the industry

Information about companies
- ★ History and current growth trends
- ★ Products and services
- ★ Financial health
- ★ Key players
- ★ Size of the workforce
- ★ Corporate environment or "culture"
- ★ Future plans

Geographic area job trends
- ★ Growth or shrinkage of the job market
- ★ Population trends or changes
- ★ Projections for the next five years
- ★ Cost-of-living factors

Where to Look
★★★

Business references and directories will be useful to you in planning your job-search strategy and researching your field. Those listed here can be found in business, public, college, and university libraries. In addition, local directories published by the Chamber of Commerce and various government agencies are available through libraries. Use all available resources in your research.

Encyclopedia of Associations—National Organizations of the U.S.
Gale Research Inc.
Book Tower
Detroit, MI 48266
3,600 pages in two volumes

Useful in locating placement committees that can help you learn of specific job openings in your field of interest, getting membership lists of individuals to develop personal contacts, and learning where and when conferences you should attend are being held.

Business Organizations, Agencies, and Publications Directory
Gale Research Inc.
Book Tower
Detroit, MI 48226
approximately 2,030 pages in two volumes

Lists business names, addresses, and contact people for approximately 24,000 organizations, as well as important publications and varied sources of data and information on all areas of business, including trade, commercial, and labor organizations, government agencies, stock exchange listings, diplomatic offices, banks, tourism, and publishing and computer information services.

Directory of U.S. Labor Organizations
BNA Books
Bureau of National Affairs, Inc.
1231 25th Street, NW
Washington, DC 20037
90 pages, biennial, fall of even years

Lists over 200 national unions and professional and state employee associations engaged in labor representation.

Consultants and Consulting Organizations Directory
Gale Research Inc.
Book Tower
Detroit, MI 48228

Lists more than 14,000 consulting organizations and individuals.

The Career Guide: Dun's Employment Opportunities Directory
Dun's Marketing Services
Dun & Bradstreet Corporation
49 Old Bloomfield Road
Mountain Lakes, NJ 07046
4,000 pages, annual November publication

Lists more than 5,000 companies that have 1,000 or more employees and that may provide career opportunities in sales, marketing, management, engineering, life and physical sciences, computer science, mathematics, statistics planning, accounting and finance, liberal arts fields, and other technical and professional areas.

The Directory of Executive Recruiters
Kennedy & Kennedy, Inc.
Templeton Road
Fitzwilliam, NH 03447
616 pages, annual

Lists over 2,000 executive recruiter firms.

America's Corporate Families: Billion Dollar Directory
Dun & Bradstreet Corporation
49 Old Bloomfield Road
Mountain Lakes, NJ 07046
approximately 10,000 pages in two volumes, annual

Identifies over 8,000 major U.S. parent companies and their subsidiaries and divisions (over 44,000).

Standard and Poor's Register of Corporations, Directors, and Executives
25 Broadway
New York, NY 10004
approximately 5,200 pages in three volumes, annual

Provides a guide to the business community with information on public companies in the United States.

Dun & Bradstreet Million Dollar Directory
Dun & Bradstreet, Inc.
3 Century Drive
Parsippany, NJ 07054
13,600 pages in 5 volumes, annual

Lists 160,000 public companies in the United States with a net worth of half a million dollars or more; includes industrial corporations, bank and trust companies, wholesales, retailers, and domestic subsidiaries of foreign corporations.

Polk's Bank Directory
North American Edition
R. L. Polk Company
2001 Elm Hill Pike
Nashville, TN 37202
3,500 pages, semiannual

Gives a major detailed listing of banks, other financial institutions, and government agencies by address.

Best's Insurance Reports, Property and Casualty
A. M. Best Company
Ambest Road
Oldwick, NJ 08858
2,200 pages, annual

Gives in-depth analyses, operating statistics, financial data and ratings, and names of officers in over 1,300 major stock and mutual property-casualty insurance companies. In addition, provides summary data on over 2,000 smaller mutual companies and on 300 casualty companies operating in Canada.

Thomas Register of American Manufacturers
Thomas Publishing Company
One Penn Plaza
New York, NY 10019
33,000 pages in 21 volumes, annual

Lists more than 140,000 specific product manufacturers. Also lists names of officers, capital assets, and parent or subsidiary companies.

Dun & Bradstreet Reference Book of Corporate Managements
Dun & Bradstreet Corporation
49 Old Bloomfield Road
Mountain Lakes, NJ 07046
3,500 pages in four volumes, annual

Contains data on nearly 200,000 presidents, officers, and managers of 12,000 credit, personnel, and data processing companies.

Developing Your Own Labor Market

You may not find the job you're seeking, especially in the area where you want to work. You have been a member of the armed forces for years; perhaps you have the itch to try something on your own. You have an idea or an invention, and it could be marketable. What do you do? What is your next step? Are the risks too high?

Eighty-five percent of all new jobs created in the past five years are not with big business but are created by people like you. It is projected that this trend will continue and even intensify. As the country continues to change to an information and service industry, there are numerous opportunities. The biggest problem with most of us is that we think the opportunity should come to us rather than have us create it.

Where to Start

★★★

If you have an entrepreneur's spirit, can afford to risk a little, and have the ability to work hard and stick to your dream, the rest is simple. Let's say you have a specialized skill that you developed prior to and during your military service, such as training others in business operations. Now, let's say that you would like to not only train others, but gather a group of other trainers to make up a consultant training network. In this instance, you want to include others in your plans because if you only market yourself, (1) you are limiting the fields of training; (2) you only make money when you are training; and (3) most clients want to hire companies, not individuals.

One of the first decisions you have to make is what kind of business you want. Consider the following options:

1. **Sole Proprietorship.** You are the only owner, and you normally market and sell only your services or products. To start a sole proprietorship is very simple. A good bookkeeper can register you in days for $500 or less. Or you can go to the nearest Secretary of State office. There are simple forms to complete, and staff are very helpful. For less than $100, you can set up your own business.

2. **Partnership.** If you have a friend who has skills, time, and financial resources, and he or she is someone you could work with, there could be some advantages to going into business together. Partners must decide what to share and what to do separately. Choosing someone who is strong in your weakest areas (such as advertising, bookkeeping, or contracting) can be a real advantage. You lose some of the control and profit, but it is often worth it.

3. **Corporation.** If you're thinking big, incorporating might be an advantage. A corporation can have many owners, investors, and employees. If your product or idea will take substantial finances to plan, develop, and market, this could be an advantage. Although it is possible for anyone to set up a corporation without an attorney, the complexity of your plans will dictate which way to go. The Secretary of State office, Small Business Administration, or even your local Chamber of Commerce can be of assistance. They all want you to make it. Corporations have additional laws, regulations, taxes, and fees that are paid to the city, state, and federal governments. You need to pay FICA, worker's compensation, franchise taxes, and so on, so it is a little more complex. Do not let this scare you off. Many husbands and wives own and operate two-person corporations and contract for all support staff and consultants.

Don't let the media or your friends fill you with myths about what it takes to start a business. Get the facts, including the following:

★ College helps, but over 40 percent of people starting businesses have only a high school diploma or less.

★ Age alone should not deter one from starting a business. Two-thirds of all new small businesses are started by people who are 30 years old or younger. You're never too young or too old.

★ Most people start their businesses near their homes.

★ Most people do not need to take out loans to start.

★ Entrepreneurs work long hours; it is not a life of leisure.

★ Most small business owners surround themselves with paid advisors (lawyer, bookkeeper, marketing expert, contracting specialists, and so on).

★ Many new businesses do not involve new products or services, but improvements on existing ones.

★ Most entrepreneurs have had some experience with being on their own, taking risks, and depending on their own talents.

If you are still thinking of going it on your own, take a personal inventory to see if you have most of the following characteristics. You do not need all of these qualities, but they are usually associated with most entrepreneurs.

★ Willing to take risks

★ Like to learn new ideas

★ Determined

★ Persistent

★ Desire to achieve

★ Need/enjoy people

★ Self-confident

★ Take failure fairly well

★ Can afford to take risks

★ Have a dream/vision

★ Good reputation

★ Like to lead

★ Self-starter

★ Never give up

★ Creative

★ Good at problem solving

★ Organized

★ Energetic

★ Good at networking

You may think of other attributes, but this gives you an idea of the qualities you will need, as well as what type of person you might consider as a partner.

Once you know what kind of business you want to start, make a list of advisors, groups, and agencies that can be of service, the following are only a few examples:

Group or Agency	*Type of Help*
American Civil Liberties Union	★ Advice on rights
U.S./local Chambers of Commerce	★ Market opportunities ★ Rules and regulations ★ Funding sources
State Department of Development	★ Funding sources ★ Marketing ★ Joint ventures
National Alliance of Business	★ Funding sources ★ Marketing ★ Joint ventures
National Clearinghouse for Legal Services	★ Specialized advice on legal issues
Women's Equity Action League	★ Rights ★ Opportunities
National Organization of Women	★ Consultation ★ Opportunities
Americans for Indian Opportunity	★ Special rights and resources
National Urban League	★ Advice on business in large cities for minorities
Workers' Defense League	★ Migrant worker information
Hispanic Institute in the U.S.	★ Hispanic opportunities
State Department of Economic Development	★ Knowledge of new market needs
State export offices	★ Export opportunities

Black Veterans Inc.	★ Special advice
American Association of Retired Persons	★ Special opportunities for those over 55 years of age
Local/state labor unions	★ Rules, costs, and benefits
Various trade associations	★ Market knowledge and worker availability
State/local employment services	★ Testing ★ Available workforce
Private industry councils	★ Tax incentives ★ Tax credits ★ Workforce

The list is endless. A few more agencies or groups that might be of assistance before or after you start your business include the following:

★ Department of Motor Vehicles   ★ Health Care Groups

★ Consumer Credit Council   ★ Insurance agents

★ Local banks   ★ Freight companies

★ Realtors (for office space)   ★ Outplacement firms

★ Printers   ★ Training institutions

★ U.S. Department of Patents   ★ U.S. Department of Copyrights

Start-up Details

★★

This section provides a basic guide for first-time business owners. It offers information as well as samples of administrative and operational techniques for small business enterprises. The information and techniques are directed at one-person businesses that have low initial start-up costs and low operational and overhead costs. There are much more detailed books and manuals on how to start a business, but the following sections summarize five key areas that are germane to all or most businesses.

Business Administration

Business administration includes general operations, product or service distribution, product or service pricing, and compliance with government regulations. Each of these areas plays an important role in your business's profitability and success.

While these areas may seem like small chores and often nuisances, your ability to manage and control them will benefit your business enterprise. They require your attention on a daily, weekly, or monthly basis; with proper planning and scheduling, you will be able to minimize inconvenience and operating costs and maximize your profits.

Banking

It is important to understand what a business checking account is and the costs of having such an account. The business checking account is different from a personal checking account in several ways, such as the size and format of the checks and deposit slips and how you write and sign the checks. Other differences are the type of service charges the bank will assess for your business account and how the bank sets up these service charges.

Banks usually require documentation regarding your business when you open up your business account. This account is used strictly for the business and should never be used as a personal checking account.

The cost of a business checking account vary from bank to bank. Some banks may offer interest-bearing business accounts. Each bank varies in what it charges for servicing a business checking account. Here are some examples of the types of charges and dollar amounts you can expect for a business checking account:

Monthly account maintenance fee	$2.75 per month
Fee for checks written on the account	$0.12 per check
Fee for deposits made to the account	$0.17 per deposit
Fee for checks included in the deposit	$0.10 per check

By establishing a good working relationship with your bank you may be able to secure loans and/or lines of credit for your business in the future. This relationship can also assist you in obtaining credit from vendors and suppliers.

Telephone Service

The telephone can be one of the most productive tools in your business. How you use it can increase or decrease your profits. Whenever you use the telephone instead of visiting your customers in person, you save time and money. You can conduct most of your business with associates and customers by using the telephone.

If your business is home-based or you want to have your business phone in your home, you will have to consider the regulations for and costs of having a business line in your home. Each state varies in its regulations and costs; complete information can be obtained from your local phone company. In most states you must have a separate phone line for business calls in your home. This is usually regulated by the Public Utilities Commission, not the phone company. Depending on the state, you may be able to substitute a business line for your residential line.

Whether you have a business phone in your home or at another site, you will have certain costs for operating it. Here is a list of the types of services you can receive and the related dollar amounts you may have to pay (these costs do not include the actual phone unit or long-distance calls, which are billed separately):

New business phone line installation	$75.00
Substitute business phone line installation	$31.15
Approximate charge for a new phone outlet installation	$42.00
Monthly service charge	$26.15 for 73 calls per month
Charge for calls over 73 per month	$0.08 per call
Service charge for touch-tone phone	$3.25 per month
FCC access rate charge for one phone line	$3.50 per month
FCC access rate charge per line for two or more phone lines	$4.16 per month
Emergency (911) service charge per phone line	$0.12 per month
Call forwarding	$3.25 per month
Call waiting	$9.60 per month
Speed calling	$3.25 per month; $5.40 per month for two lines
Business line transfer	$0.80 per month

The phone company surveyed for these charges also offers a small business package. The charges vary depending on which options you buy and how many phone lines and units you operate. Some of the services provided by this package include the following:

- ★ Speed calling
- ★ Call forwarding
- ★ Call on hold
- ★ Conference calling
- ★ Call pick-up
- ★ Call waiting
- ★ Alternate answering
- ★ Intercom system
- ★ Call transfer

If you hire an answering service for your business venture, here are some of the services and related costs a typical service business will charge:

Answering a common line for all businesses in the service	$30.00 per month
Answering your business line separately (Both services are for 40 calls per month; over 40 calls, $0.20 per call)	$40.00 per month
Providing a mail box with a street address instead of a box number	$12.00 per month
Receiving fax transmissions	$2.00 per page
Sending fax transmissions	$2.00 to $4.00 per page, plus $0.50 per minute
Typing	$2.50 to $5.00 per page

If your decide to purchase an answering machine, you can expect to pay $34.97 to $149.97 at a reasonable store.

Scheduling

Using a wall, pocket, or desk calendar with space to schedule for each day is one of the most important procedures in running a profitable business. Keeping track of tasks and appointments can keep you on top of the daily, weekly, and monthly business administration duties necessary to operate your firm.

Some of the necessary items and tasks you need to schedule and plan for, including the average time each task should take, are as follows:

Paying bills and loan payments	1 to 2 hours per week
Making bank deposits	½ to 1 hour per day
Balancing checkbook	1 to 2 hours per month
Paying and/or depositing payroll, sales, and other taxes	1 to 2 hours per month
Reviewing and revising cash budget	1 to 2 hours per week
Making customer sales calls	minimum of 2 hours per day
Reviewing customer sales calls	1 to 2 hours per week
Making deliveries of products and services	depends on customer demand
Inventorying supplies and merchandise	1 to 2 hours per month
Ordering supplies and merchandise	½ to 1 hour per week
Receiving deliveries and/or making pick-ups of supplies or merchandise	1 to 4 hours per week
Making and keeping appointments with customers, associates, and vendors/suppliers	depends on customer demand; 1 to 4 hours per week for associates and vendors/suppliers
Creating job and work schedules	1 to 2 hours per week

Resources

Exhibit 12.1 is a list of reference books, magazines, and newspapers that will be helpful in finding vendors, suppliers, trade information about your industry, financial information, basic business news, and, perhaps, customers. (Other marketing methods are mentioned in the "Marketing and Sales" section of this chapter.)

You will find most of these reference books, magazines, and newspapers in your public library and the local college or university library (if the college or university has a business department, college, or school, there may also be a business library). Many of the magazines and newspapers listed can be obtained through a subscription. When using a library, always consult the librarian for additional reference books, publications, and materials.

EXHIBIT 12.1
Resources for Beginning Entrepreneurs

Reference Books   *Reviewed*

The Thomas Register
  (product information for North American
  manufacturing companies)   _____

Local and regional telephone books
  (business telephone listings)   _____

Encyclopedia of Associations
  (listing of trade and business associations)   _____

National Trade and Professional Associations of the U.S.
  (listing of trade and professional associations)   _____

Harris Directories
  (listing of manufacturing companies in all 50 states)   _____

Brands and Their Companies
  (consumer products and their manufacturers)   _____

Dun & Bradstreet's Million Dollar Directory
  (business information on companies with $500,000 plus
  net worth)   _____

Standard & Poor's Register of Corporations
  (important business facts on corporations with
  $1,000,000 plus sales)   _____

Standard & Poor's Industry Surveys
  (basic and current analysis of all major domestic
  industries)   _____

Standard Directory of Advertisers
  (listing of companies that place national and regional
  advertising)   _____

Worldscope Financial and Service Company Profile
  (comparative financial investment data)   _____

Ward's Business Directory
  (listing of 85,000 companies' information by sales and
  industry activity)   _____

continued

Local Chamber of Commerce's membership directory   _____
   (listing of local and regional businesses that are chamber
   members)

Predicasts F&S Index   _____
   (national and international companies' product and
   industry information)

Predicasts' Basebook   _____
   (industries' statistical abstracts)

Predicasts Forecasts   _____
   (abstracts of published forecasts for the United States)

RMA Annual Statement Studies   _____
   (composite financial data on industries' lines of business)

The U.S. Industrial Outlook   _____
   (U.S. Department of Commerce economic predictions)

U.S. Department of Commerce Bureau of Census Economic   _____
Census
   (major source of facts about nature and structure of
   U.S. economy)

U.S. Department of Commerce Bureau of Census Census of   _____
Population
   (social and economic characteristics of U.S. residents)

U.S. Department of Commerce Bureau of Census County   _____
Business Patterns
   (annual series of state and national publications
   presenting data on the number of establishments, total
   employment, and payroll on an establishment basis by
   county in each state)

National Publications   *Reviewed*

Business Week   _____

Inc.   _____

Fortune   _____

Forbes   _____

Barron's   _____

Wall Street Journal   _____

continued

New York Times _____

Success _____

Time _____

Newsweek _____

Christian Science Monitor _____

Washington Post _____

Los Angeles Times _____

Sales and Marketing Management _____

Other Resources   *Reviewed*

Regional or district office of the U.S. Small Business   _____
Administration (SBA)

Local office of SCORE or ACE, SBA-sponsored business   _____
counselor volunteers

U.S. Department of Commerce Field Office   _____

Local Chamber of Commerce office   _____

Nearest office of the Better Business Bureau   _____

Local government offices for permits, building and zoning   _____
codes, and sales tax information

Local city or county Economic or Industrial Development   _____
Service office

The nearest Small Business Development Center (SBDC),   _____
an SBA co-sponsored counseling and training center

Product or Service Pricing

Developing a pricing schedule for your products or services can be a difficult task. There are many formulas and methods, but the important issues are as follows:

★ How much will your customer be willing to pay for your product or service?

★ Will you make a profit from your selling price?

You must be competitive in pricing. Often, when you are just starting your business, you will ask a price lower than the competition's so you can enter the market. You should be able to call and find out from local competition what they are charging for their products and services. Other methods of marketing research are discussed in the ''Marketing and Sales'' section.

When you have found out what the competition is charging and what the standard prices for your products or services are, you must decide what you will charge. Some questions to ask yourself are:

★ Is my quality the same, better, or worse than the standard for my product or service?

★ Can I enter the marketplace at the standard price, or should I lower my prices at first and the slowly raise them as I find more customers?

★ Will I make a profit with these prices?

To figure out whether you will make a profit with prospective prices, you must analyze the costs you will incur in making and delivering your products and services. When determining your costs, you must consider the following components:

★ Labor costs

★ Material costs

★ Overhead costs

If you are a sole proprietor, you must consider your labor cost. A reasonable way of determining this cost is, what would your wages be if you were to perform this service or manufacture this product for someone else? To this amount, you must add on payroll taxes for social security, workers' compensation, insurance, and unemployment tax contributions.

Material costs include the actual cost of any and all materials you use in the delivery of your service or manufacture of your products. Included in these costs should be any sales tax you had to pay (in most states, if you are reselling a product, you can be exempt from sales tax), any and all freight to your business, and freight you had to pay to ship to your customer. When possible, you should add in a waste factor for materials, especially if you are manufacturing products.

Overhead costs to consider include the following:

★ Rent

★ Supplies

★ Loan payments

★ Equipment rentals and costs

★ Utilities

★ Outside services

★ Taxes

★ Car and/or truck expenses

★ Telephone

★ Insurance

★ Advertising and sales costs

When you have calculated your costs for labor, material, and overhead, you should develop a price for your service and product known as a markup. Marking up your costs lets you determine a price for your product or service that is competitive and still allows you to make a reasonable profit. The final price should be one that your customers are willing to pay, that will cover your costs of doing business, and that gives you a profit.

Government Regulations

When beginning your business enterprise, you must be aware of the licenses, permits, and tax obligations you will be responsible for obtaining and paying. Much of the information concerning these items can be obtained by contacting your local SBDC sub-center, the district or regional office of the SBA, or the local office of SCORE.

Permits and Licenses

Federal.   Although there are no regular federal permits or licenses needed for most small businesses, if you want to contract with a federal agency, you will have to qualify yourself as a legitimate supplier or contractor before you can bid and conduct business. In addition, if you deal in areas that are regulated by the federal government, for example, communications, agriculture, food and drugs, medical-related products, environmentally hazardous materials, or interstate commerce, you must meet federal licensing requirements. It is important to investigate any federal agency that regulates your industry before you start your business.

State.   Most states have similar regulations for operating businesses regardless of size. Many states require licensing for construction and trade businesses and individuals, and also have licensing requirements for food preparation, handling, and delivery, as well as transportation and agriculture.

Your state may require you to register your business concern or company as a corporation, sole proprietorship, or some form of a partnership.

It is important to contact the state agencies that require permits and licenses and that may regulate your industry.

County and local.   Most county and/or city government agencies require you to obtain a basic business or vendor's license to operate within the county or city limits. In addition, they may have requirements for commercial, industrial, and residential building zones, as well as conditions regarding construction, trade, and food-related businesses.

Taxes

Federal

One of the first steps in opening your business enterprise will be to acquire a federal tax identification number. Your own social security number may be used if you are a sole proprietor. This process makes you liable for federal unemployment, withholding, social security, and corporation/company income tax. Contact your local Internal Revenue Service office to acquire the identification number and receive information about the federal tax process.

State

In addition to contacting the Internal Revenue Service, you must contact the state revenue or tax office, and/or the state corporation and/or secretary of state office. From them, you can get information about registering your business at the state level and starting the process for dealing with state taxes for unemployment, corporation/company income, withholding and sales. You must also contact the state agency responsible for workers' compensation to see if your type or size of business must pay for this insurance.

County and Local

Many counties and cities also have requirements for withholding and sales taxes. Contact the county and city offices for information regarding these tax regulations. There may be property taxes for equipment, machinery, inventory, and vehicles being used for business purposes.

Marketing and Sales

The key to your successful business is based on your ability to market your products or services. You must be able to find, contact, and approach your customers, and sell your products or services to that customer. You need marketing and sales skills to make your business a successful and profitable venture. You are the person who knows best how the products and services work and how the customer can use these products and services most effectively.

Marketing Research

Before marketing your products and services, ask yourself the following questions:

★ How good is your idea for your products and services?

★ Do your potential customers know how good your idea is?

★ Where are these customers located, and how can you reach them?

★ How much will they pay for your product or service?

★ Is there any competition? If so, who is the competition, and where are they located?

★ Are there any local, state, or federal regulations concerning your business operations that may limit your ability to sell your product or service?

To answer these questions, you must do some marketing research. The initial part of your research should deal with the industry in which your company will operate. For example, if you are a pushcart food vendor, you are in the food service industry; if your business is home building, you are in the construction industry. By researching your industry, you can obtain the following types of useful information:

★ Current trends in your customers' buying habits

★ Current products and services being offered to customers

★ Suppliers of equipment and materials for your industry

★ Current sales and profits for other companies in your industry

★ Competitors and where they are located

★ Marketing strategies being used by other companies in your industry

★ The newest tools, materials, and equipment developed by and for your industry

This information, in turn, will give you some basic marketing knowledge in these areas:

★ Product and service pricing

★ Sales techniques to use with your customers

★ The best-selling products and services to offer your customers

★ Advantages you may have over your competitors and those the competitors have over you

★ A comparison of your products and services to others in the industry

The information you gathered about your industry will also help in your budgeting process, in preparing a start-up list of tools, equipment, and materials, and in determining where you might locate your business.

Information about your industry is available in many of the resource materials listed in the "Resources" section of this chapter. Let's recap where you can find these materials:

★ **Public libraries.** All libraries have some information regarding business. In larger libraries, there may be a business division or section. You will find directories, reference materials, and books to assist you in marketing and industry research.

- ★ **College or university libraries.** Colleges or universities may have a separate library for business; at the least, they will have a business section in the main campus library. They will have many of the same types of materials and books a public library has, probably more.

- ★ **Associations.** Associations related to your industry will have a lot of information you can use. Attending local, regional, and national conventions and meetings can also be beneficial. A list of associations can be found in the reference section of most libraries. Ask the librarian for help.

- ★ **Franchisors.** If your industry is involved with franchising, write to major franchisors for information.

Labor

Your labor and the labor of an employee cost more than the hourly wage you actually pay yourself and that employee. To do a proper estimate of labor costs, you will have to consider the hourly wage, the number of hours of work each year, the FICA (Social Security Tax), the state unemployment tax, the federal unemployment tax, workers' compensation insurance or other insurance costs, and any other labor cost.

In most states, employers are required by law to carry workers' compensation coverage for their full-time and part-time employees. The rates for coverage are set by each state according to specific job classifications. For example, if you are a service company doing carpentry work, your rate will be higher than if you are a service company doing secretarial work in your home. Whether your business is a sole proprietorship, partnership, or corporation, your business is liable for workers' compensation coverage.

You are also responsible for paying state unemployment insurance premiums for yourself and employees, and you are assigned a minimum rate.

You can determine your labor costs by using a labor cost sheet. The following are sample entries for such a form:

- ★ Laborer (you, full- and part-time employees, subcontractors)

- ★ Hourly wage rate ($10.00; $8.00; $5.00; and $12.00 per hour, respectively)

- ★ Yearly hours (2,080 hours; 52 weeks times 40 hours a week; 1,000 hours; and 100 hours, respectively)

- ★ Yearly salary (hourly wage rate times the yearly hours)

- ★ FICA (7.65% or .0765 times the yearly salary)

★ State unemployment (5.1% or .051 times the yearly salary)

★ Federal unemployment (0.8% or .008 times the yearly salary)

★ Workers' compensation (12% or. 12 times the yearly salary)

★ Other labor costs (other insurance costs or local payroll tax on labor)

★ Total labor cost (the sum of yearly salary, FICA, state unemployment, federal unemployment, workers' compensation, and other labor costs)

★ Yearly hours available (1,976 hours [there are 2,080 possible work hours per year, but for this example we subtracted 104 hours for eight holidays and five vacation days]; 1,000 hours for the part-time employee; and 100 hours for the subcontractor)

★ Hourly wage cost (the actual hourly labor cost for estimating purposes. The cost is determined by dividing the dollar amount in the total labor cost column by the number of hours in the yearly hours available column.)

Moving On
★★

Other issues like estimating, inventory merchandising, work schedules, accounting, and so on, are important to the running and growth of your business, but are beyond the scope of this book. If you decide to start your own business, there are many more detailed guides available to help you.

Networking

No matter where you are moving, or what type of career you plan to pursue, you will find a similar set of available resources to help with your short- and long-term transition. As we discussed in Chapter 10, knowing and using human and organizational resources are by far the best means of connecting with obvious and hidden labor markets. It is predicted that over 70 percent of the labor market could best be accessed by networking with support groups. An expert job hunter will systematically identify, keep records of, and use these networks as needed.

Starting Your Network
★★

Family and friends represent the surest and most efficient network if you are moving to a city near them. They also have extended family and friends who, if orchestrated effectively, can be quite far-reaching.

If you have former teachers, instructors, and employers or supervisors living in your new home location, they too can be useful. Besides knowing you well, they have insights and networks within the hidden labor market, and they can make productive contacts with employers on your behalf. Don't be afraid to ask. Most people are flattered to be asked, but you must take the first step.

In all communities there are private and public groups that help with job placement. You will meet them at employment agencies, the unemployment office, a school's placement bureau, and personnel offices. These people are a good source of current information about job openings and job-hunting techniques. Introduce yourself to fellow job-hunters and share your experiences with them. Although chances are your career interests are quite different, they may be able to provide you with information relevant to your job search and give you the names of individuals you might contact for help. They also may be able to suggest job-search techniques they are using that you haven't considered yet. You should view and use other job-hunters as contacts with whom you can exchange information.

The phone book is a critical tool in establishing and maintaining a contact network. If you do not have the one for the area in which you are seeking employment, you can obtain a copy at a business library or from the phone company itself.

Use the yellow pages to find the names of businesses who employ people in your field of interest. You do not need the name of a specific individual, only the knowledge that a position requiring your skills and abilities exists in the company you are calling. Ask to speak to the person who holds the position and request their help in getting information about your field of choice.

Telephone books can serve two major purposes:

1. To develop a list of all businesses that employ people in your field of interest.

2. To determine the location where you may find your ideal job. You may want to use more than one city directory to increase your options.

Finding Your Contacts
★★

Let's look at some specific groups and techniques for you to explore.

Former Classmates

Many of the people you were in classes and other activities with, may have unique keys to employment opportunities. Call your high school, college, or university to get a directory of addresses for your old classmates. Some directories also tell you what your old friends are doing, and you find that some of them are in hiring positions. Having connections with someone on the inside can help. Don't forget, even if you went to college in one city, it may have alumni groups all over the country.

Employment Offices

Your taxes pay for employment specialists, and help is yours for the asking. The public (jobs) employment office has the following resources:

★ Job counselors—who know the local/state job market

★ Free tests and inventories, and their interpretation

★ Part-time job listings

★ Full-time job listings

★ Placement interview assistance

★ Recommended training opportunities and financial aid

★ Many useful brochures and booklets to help in your transition preparation

There also are a host of private placement agencies in your yellow pages, which usually come in three types:

1. Those that offer only career counseling, for which you pay.

2. Self-placement readiness centers for nonprofessional careers and for which you pay.

3. Headhunters who have contracts with corporations and who are always in search of available talent. They usually get paid by the employer who hires you so the risk to you is reduced.

Be careful when shopping for transition help. Check out several options before you sign a contract. Most of the "pay-as-you-go" agencies never promise employment. You need to decide how much it's worth to get close to employers and then sell yourself through interviews and impeccable credentials.

Become well known at some of the public employment offices for they often operate with an out-of-sight-out-of-mind philosophy. Be a friendly pest—they should recognize you by name when you walk in.

Unearthing the Hidden Labor Market
★★

It's possible that 80 percent of all jobs today are not listed anywhere. So, how do you find them? You will need to use a "person-next-door" approach to get a better feel for the real opportunities.

Church

Check with the church office or rectory to see if they have a directory of the congregation. Usually the directory will tell you who works where and who owns or runs what company. What better connection then to say, "I go to church with you, and I see you work at XYZ company. I'm a veteran just returning home and need some help."

Bank

When you open your accounts, get a mortgage, and so on, ask to see the branch manager. Tell him or her what you are looking for. They are in contact with the local economy and might give you hints as to who is expanding, coming to town, or hiring.

Newspaper

If it's true that only 12 to 15 percent of all job openings are listed in the want ads, buy some space and advertise yourself. Don't wait for the employer; declare your availability and employability.

Clubs

Decide what club or two in town has the most employers in it and begin to systematically work the crowd. The Lions, Chamber, Sertoma, National Guard, Reserves, or any other social or civic clubs are all good bets.

Family

You've just returned home, so you have a good excuse (opportunity) to write or call relatives to say, "Hello, I'm home. I'm looking for work, and I need help." You'll never know how many of your extended family members are well connected until you try them.

Cold Mailings

Although a little time consuming, you could select 15 to 25 employers in your field, find out personnel directors' names, prepare a customized letter, include your resumé and credentials, and let them know you're home and available. Realize that veterans are valued potential employees because of their previous military training and service. After a week or two, call and try to arrange an appointment.

Volunteering

In some fields, you might stimulate interest by saying you'll work free for a certain number of days to demonstrate your skills and productivity. Additionally, volunteering at churches, shelters, community events, schools, and so forth could allow you to get close to key people. When you work the employment field this way, you never know who you will meet tomorrow.

Summary

★★

Use the system, existing networks, and every contact you have. Besides finding good employment, it will put you in touch with many people you should be contacting anyway. No matter how big or small your network is, keep track of your contacts. None of us can remember everything, so keep a log. Such as the one in Exhibit 13.1. The last section of the chapter lists names and addresses of groups, agencies, and organizations that could come in handy.

EXHIBIT 13.1

Support Network Information Log

Contact Name and Title	Phone	Company Name and Address	Purpose in Contacting	Date of Contact	Comment/Follow-up Needed	Information Supplied (Them/Me)
1.						
2.						
3.						
4.						
5.						
6.						
7.						
8.						
9.						
10.						
11.						

Targeted National Groups for Possible Networking and Assistance

Aging

American Association of Retired
Persons
1909 K St, NW
Washington DC 20049

Legal Counsel for the Elderly
1909 K Street, NW
Washington DC 20049

National Clearinghouse on Aging
Administration on Aging
330 Independence Ave., SW
Washington, DC 20201

National Council on the Aging
600 Maryland Ave., SW
West Wing 100
Washington, DC 20024

National Institute of Senior Centers
c/o National Council on the Aging
600 Maryland Ave, SW
West Wing 100
Washington, DC 20024

Urban Elderly Coalition
600 Maryland Ave., SW
West Wing 204
Washington, DC 20024

Appalachians

Appalachia Educational Laboratory
P.O. Box 1348
Charleston, WV 25325

Appalachian Regional Commission
1666 Connecticut Ave., NW
Washington, DC 20235

Asian Americans

Asian American Legal Defense and
Education Fund
99 Hudson St., 12th Floor
New York, NY 10013

Department of Health and Human
Services
Division of Asian American Affairs
200 Independence Ave., SW
Room 419E Hubert Humphrey Bldg.
Washington, DC 20201

Japanese American Citizens League
1765 Sutter St.
San Francisco, CA 94115

National Pacific Asian Resource
Center on Aging
811 First Ave., Suite 210
Seattle, WA 98104

Organization of Chinese Americans
2025 Eye St., NW
Suite No. 926
Washington, DC 20006

Vietnam Foundation
6713 Lumsden St.
McLean, VA 22101

Black Americans

Alpha Kappa Alpha
5656 S. Stony Island Ave.
Chicago, IL 30637

Alpha Phi Alpha
4432 Martin Luther King Dr.
Chicago, IL 60653

Black Veterans, Inc.
1119 Fulton St.
Brooklyn, NY 11238

Delta Sigma Theta
1707 New Hampshire Ave., NW
Washington, DC 20009

National Association for the
Advancement of Colored People
186 Remsen St.
Brooklyn, NY 11201

National Urban League
500 E. 62nd St.
New York, NY 10021

Dislocated Workers

Human Resources Development
Institute (AFL-CIO)
815 16th St., NW
Washington, DC 20006

Labor Management Services
Administration
U.S. Department of Labor
200 Constitution Avenue, NW
Washington, DC 20210

National Association of Counties
440 First St., NW
Washington, DC 20001

National Governors' Association
444 North Capitol St., NW
Washington, DC 20001

Handicapped

American Council of the Blind
1211 Connecticut Ave., NW
Suite 506
Washington, DC 20036

American Deafness and
Rehabilitation Association
814 Thayer Ave.
Silver Spring, MD 20910

American Speech-Language-Hearing
Association
10801 Rockville Pike
Rockville, MD 20852

Association for Education and
Rehabilitation of the Blind and
Visually Handicapped
206 W. Washington St., Suite 320
Alexandria, VA 22314

Goodwill Industries of America
9200 Wisconsin Ave.
Bethesda, MD 20814

Information Center for Individuals
with Disabilities
20 Park Plaza, Rm. 330
Boston, MA 02116

National Association of the Deaf
814 Thayer Ave.
Silver Spring, MD 20901

National Association for Visually
Handicapped
305 E. 24th St., 17-C
New York, Ny 10010

National Easter Seal Society
2023 W. Ogden Ave.
Chicago, Il 60612

Presidents Committee on
Employment of the Handicapped
Washington, DC 20210

Hispanic

ASPIRA of America
114 E. 28th St.
New York, NY 10016

Chicano Training Center
7145 Avenue H
Houston, TX 77011

Mexican American Legal Defense
and Educational Fund (MALDEF)
28 Geary
San Francisco, CA 94108

National Coalition of Hispanic
Mental Health and Human Services
Organization
1030 15th St., NW
Suite 1053
Washington, DC 20005

National Council of La Raza
20 F St., 2nd Fl.
Washington, DC 20001

Hispanic Public Affairs Association
P.O. Box 5488
Friendship Heights Station
Washington, DC 20016

Mexican-American Opportunity
Foundation
670 Monterey Pass Rd.
Monterey Park, CA 91754

National Puerto Rican Forum
450 Park Ave., S.
New York, NY 10016

Limited English

National Association for Bilingual
Education
1201 16th St., NW
Room 405
Washington, DC 20036

National Clearinghouse for Bilingual
Education
1555 Wilson Blvd., Suite 605
Rosslyn, VA 22209

Regional Bilingual Training
Resource Center
City of New York Board of
Education
Center for Bilingual Education
110 Livingston St., Rm. 224
Brooklyn, NY 11202

Native Americans

Americans for Indian Opportunity
1140 Connecticut Avenue, NW
Suite 301
Washington, DC 20036

Bureau of Indian Affairs
1951 Constitution Ave., NW
Washington, DC 20245

Bureau of Indian Affairs
Office of Indian Education
Programs
Indian Education Resources Center
Box 1788
Albuquerque, NM 87103

National Congress of American
Indians
804 D St., NE
Washington, DC 20002

National Indian Education
Association
1115 Second Ave., S
Minneapolis, MN 55403

National Indian Training and
Research Center
2121 S. Mill Ave., Suite 218
Tempe, AZ 85282

National Urban Indian Council
2258 S. Broadway
Denver, CO 80210

North American Indian Association
360 John R
Detroit, MI 48226

Office of Indian Opportunity
Referral Center
1410 E. Forty-sixth St., N
Tulsa, OK 74126

United Native Americans
7787 Earl Ct.
El Cerrito, CA 94530

Rural

Farmers Home Administration
U.S. Department of Agriculture
Washington, DC 20250

Green Thumb
1401 Wilson Blvd., Suite 108
Arlington, VA 22209

Housing Assistance Council
1025 Vermont Ave., NW
Suite 606
Washington, DC 20005

Office of Fair Housing and Equal
Opportunity, Housing and Urban
Development
Washington, DC 20410

Single Parents

Parent Support-Group Project
294 Washington St., Suite 630
Boston, MA 02108

Parents Without Partners
7910 Woodmont Ave., Suite 1000
Bethesda, MD 20814

Veterans

Disabled American Veterans
3725 Alexandria Pike
Cold Spring, KY 41076

National Veteran's Outreach
Program
1017 N. Main, Suite 200
San Antonio, TX 78212

Veterans Education Project
P.O. Box 42130
Washington, DC 20015

Vietnam Veterans Agent Orange
Victims
93 Prospect St.
Stamford, CT 06902

Vietnam Veterans of America
1133 Broadway
New York, NY 10010

Vietnam Veterans Institute for
Research and Advocacy
1700 K St., NW
Suite 503
Washington, DC 20005

Vietnam Veterans Leadership
Program
806 Connecticut Ave., NW
Washington, DC 20525

Vocational Rehabilitation for
Disabled Veterans
Veterans Administration
810 Vermont Ave., NW
Washington, DC 20420

Women

Advocates for Women
414 Mason St.
San Francisco, CA 94102

National Organization for Women
425 13th St., NW, Suite 723
Washington, DC 20004

National Womens' Employment
and Education
P.O. Box 959
118 N. Broadway, Suite 622
San Antonio, TX 78294

Tradeswomen
P.O. Box 40664
San Francisco, CA 94140

Wider Opportunities for Women
1325 G St., NW
Lower Level
Washington, DC 20005

Women Employed
Five S. Wabash, Suite 415
Chicago, IL 60603

Women's Equity Action League
805 15th St., NW
Suite 822
Washington, DC 20005

General Services Providers

Al-Anon Family Group
Headquarters
One Park Ave.
New York, NY 10016

Alcoholics Anonymous World
Service
P.O. Box 459
Grand Central Station
New York, NY 10163

American Civil Liberties Union
132 W. 43rd St.
New York, NY 10036

Chamber of Commerce of the U.S.
1615 H St., NW
Washington, DC 20062

National Alliance of Business
1015 15th St., NW
Washington, DC 20005

National Association of Private
Industry Councils
1201 New York Ave., NW
Suite 800
Washington, DC 20005

National Association of Recovered
Alcoholics
P.O. Box 95
Staten Island, NY 10305

National Association on Drug
Abuse Problems
355 Lexington Ave.
New York, NY 10017

National Clearinghouse for Drug
Abuse Information
National Institute of Drug Abuse,
Alcohol, Drug Abuse, and Mental
Health Administration
5600 Fishers Lane, Rm. 10-A53
Rockville, MD 20857

National Clearinghouse for Legal
Services
407 S. Dearborn, Suite 400
Chicago, IL 60605

National Coalition for the
Homeless
105 E. 22nd St.
New York, NY 10010

National Council on Alcoholism
733 Third Ave.
New York, NY 10017

Opportunities Industrialization
Centers of America
100 W. Coulter St.
Philadelphia, PA 19144

Salvation Army
799 Bloomfield Ave.
Verona, NJ 07044

Transitional Case Studies

Much of our emphasis until now has been on gaining a better understanding of the world in which you will live after you leave military service. Now it's time to focus on what you might want to do in that world, where *not* working is a luxury few can afford.

The first steps in the transition process are similar for everyone: Establish an objective; inventory the skills and personal resources that will help you meet that objective; set up alternative courses of acton to reach the objective; and then decide on the course of action that offers the best possibility of reaching the objective.

If that reads a bit like a tactical "estimate of the situation," it's supposed to. There is no reason why you should abandon the problem-solving techniques you have learned during military service just because you are leaving the military environment. Those techniques can work for you wherever you go. Don't ever forget that a valuable personal asset on the job is your ability to solve problems. The first evidence of that ability is how you set about launching your civilian career.

In the final analysis, you are the only one who can solve the problems involved in your own transition. Guidelines can be provided. Sources of assistance can be pointed out. But before you are ready to hang up that uniform for the last time, you have a lot of work ahead of you.

What problems are involved in the transition process? They center around the development of realistic career objectives, problems that are more easily stated than solved. For example:

1. Establishing an objective

   ★ What do I want to do for the rest of my life?

   ★ In what industry or business should I seek a job?

   ★ How much time do I need to prepare myself? How much time do I have?

2. Inventorying skills, personal resources, and other factors

   ★ What skills are required for employment?

   ★ What skills or experience do I already have?

   ★ What favorable personal traits do I have?

   ★ What personal assets and liabilities (financial status, education, family, geographical location, physical condition, and so on) can or will influence my objective?

   ★ What physical conditions (heat, cold, dust, noise, health hazards, and so on) am I likely to encounter on the job?

3. Identifying some possible courses of action

   ★ Leave service as soon as I'm eligible; seek immediate employment in a special field in which I'm already trained.

   ★ Remain in service (reenlist/extend tour, if necessary); seek advanced training, education, and experience required for civilian employment in my current occupational field.

   ★ Leave service; abandon military specialty; seek retraining in civilian institution to prepare for an unrelated job.

   ★ Remain in service (reenlist/extend tour); seek new military specialization; acquire advanced training and improve my general educational level.

Which of the possible courses of action you may eventually pursue depends on you. You may develop others, in fact, to suit your own circumstances. One course you should not even consider: "Leave service as soon as I can; I'll find *something, somewhere*." Forget it! Employers, you may recall, want employees who are highly motivated and who enthusiastically identify with the employer's objectives. That brings you right back to the beginning: What is your career objective? If you do not have an objective, it is time to think about one.

As you work through your transition planning you should keep these factors in mind. As a general rule, the *competition* for jobs in a slow-growing occupation is greater than in a field that is growing faster than the average. Conversely, the *average pay* in the slow-growing occupational field may be lower than in the field that is growing faster, in accordance with the economic law of supply and demand.

The "fast-track" occupations are the fields in which the numbers of new jobs are expected to grow faster than the national average and to continue to grow in the future. If you are already trained and working in one of these fields in military service, you are probably ahead of the game. If you are not, you may want to give serious consideration to preparing yourself for one of them while you are still in the service, because they are the jobs of the future.

That does not mean, of course, that there won't be other opportunities for employment. Heed, however, the plight of the young apprentice buggymaker at the turn of the century when automobiles were just appearing. He not only had to adjust to an environment that was changing rapidly in response to new technology, but he had to change his occupation in midlife. Today, thousands of jobs in a couple of hundred occupational fields are endangered by shifting trends and new technology.

Evaluating Your Military Training and Experience
★★★

One of the most useful places to begin researching the marketability of your military training and experience is the *Occupational Outlook Handbook*. You can find the *Handbook* in the reference section of the library at most military bases and in almost any public library; you may also find that your base education center has a copy. If you can't find a copy on the base, ask the librarian or the education center director to order one. Or order a copy yourself from a publisher such as VGM Career Horizons. The publication sells for less than $20 and is well worth the price. It contains detailed descriptions of about 200 civilian occupations or career fields that provide employment for about 60 percent of the civilian labor force. They include about 90 percent of the technical and professional specialties that are expected to provide increasing employment opportunities through 1995 and probably beyond. Briefer comments on 200 other career fields are included in an appendix.

The main purpose of the *Occupational Outlook Handbook* is to discuss the occupational fields in which about 60 percent of the members of the civilian workforce are employed. It is interesting to note that about 58 percent of the *Dictionary of Occupational Titles* (DOT) job titles attributed to enlisted military occupations are included in that section. Another 19 percent are included in the summary appendix; these titles include various clerical jobs, boat operators, blasters (demolition experts), seamen, shipfitters, shipping and receiving clerks, and stock and inventory specialists. That leaves about a quarter of the DOT job titles unaccounted for, but they are largely concerned with such military specialties as intelligence, emergency management, electronic weapon repairers, and ordinance specialties that have bona fide civilian counterparts but do not occupy a significant portion of the civilian workforce. (Jobs of this kind are most likely to be found in the federal civil service or among defense contractors.) If you are in a job field that is not included in the main body of the *Handbook,* you can find details of the civilian jobs in your field in the *Dictionary of Occupation Titles,* which includes training requirements in its listings.

The narrative descriptions of the 200 or so occupational fields in the *Handbook* are invaluable as an introduction to civilian training standards and work requirements, whether you are an E-4 automobile mechanic or an O-5 combat commander rounding out 20 years of military service. The information is especially valuable to career combat arms officers and enlisted men who are considering alternative military specialties or changing military occupational specialities. Given the opportunity, why not select a new miltary specialty that may later help you move into a civilian occupation? Or you may simply want to evaluate your accumulative military training and experience, professional military education, or civilian education against the standards in the *Handbook* for civilian occupations. A timely review of this kind can allow you to take action to supplement any deficiencies while you're still in service by taking advantage of opportunities for training, education, and assignments that might otherwise be overlooked.

Taking the Statistical Approach

We should look at another Department of Labor publication that is published each year as a statistical supplement to the *Occupational Outlook Handbook.* The title is *Occupational Projections and Training Data.* You may be able to find a copy at a base Education Center or a good public library; or you may be able to talk your base librarian into ordering a copy for the reference collection.

Occupational Projections and Training Data contains brief statistical summaries that augment the narrative material in the *Handbook.* It is full of statistics but fairly easy to work with. Short descriptive sections are included, but they are not as useful as the detailed narratives in the *Handbook.* These statistical summaries provide useful information that can help you with career decisions. The amount of information varies by occupational field, but a typical summary includes the following:

★ **Employment profile:** Total employment in the field, selected characteristics of workers (sex, race, age, number of part-time employees), unemployment rate, industry concentration of workers, projected employment, employment growth, and annual separation rate (percent of employees leaving their jobs). *Note:* Projected jobs are given in three categories: low, moderate, and high. This is the Department of Labor's way of hedging for possible recessions or economic slowdowns. ''Moderate growth'' is the category used by most people to attempt to predict future employment.

★ **Supply profile:** Entry and training requirements, training completions (numbers of students who completed training in various kinds of institutions), and characteristics of entrants.

Case Study: *Researching Civilian Employment Standards*

Jim is an Army E-4 who enlisted after graduating from high school with a general diploma. He has been working for about a year and a half as a light vehicle auto mechanic gaining on-the-job training after completing an entry-level Army technical school at the top of his class. Recently he has begun to specialize in transmissions. He enjoys the work and is good at it, but he really wants to leave the Army in about a year, when his enlistment is up. His high school sweetheart, Jean, is waiting for him.

Jim's Objectives. To get a second job as a transmission mechanic; work hard to get ahead; advance to service manager; eventually set up his own shop; settle down to raise a family.

Jim's Possible Courses of Action.

1. Leave the Army when his enlistment expires; find a job as a transmission mechanic; marry Jean!

2. Leave Army when his enlistment expires; find any job; marry Jean?

3. Reenlist in the Army; seek advanced technical training; master skills; become a shop supervisor. What about Jean?

Jim wonders what kind of job he might be able to get in the automotive field with the training and experience he will have at the end of his three-year enlistment. He starts by looking up the military occupation of automobile mechanics in the *Occupational Outlook Handbook*. He finds four DOT job classifications under the military occupation of ''automobile mechanics.''

620261010	Automobile Mechanic	F HBK
620281034	Carburetor Mechanic	F HBK
620281034	Transmission Mechanic	F HBK
620381010	Automobile Radiator Mechanic	F HBK

According to the letter codes, all four jobs are on the fast track. The *Handbook* includes a discussion of each occupation, but where does Jim find the one he wants in the 500-plus page *Handbook?*

At the back of the *Handbook* is the "Index of Occupations." He looks under "Transmission Mechanic" to find the correct page number. When he turns to that page, he finds that "Transmission Mechanic" is included in a general discussion of "Automotive and Motorcycle Mechanics." It is important at this point to understand that the *Handbook* narratives describe occupational fields, not *jobs* in the narrow sense of the term.

Jim also discovers that each narrative description of a civilian occupation in the *Handbook* has the same organization, with the following subject headings and content:

Nature of the Work. What you are expected to do; what you are expected to know.

Working Conditions. Environmental considerations (indoors/outdoors, noise levels, temperatures), physical requirements, health hazards, safety considerations, and so forth.

Employment. How many people work in the field; where they are employed.

Training, Other Qualifications, and Advancement. Training standards, certification procedures, essential personal traits, opportunities for promotion.

Job Outlook. Relative growth expected in the number of jobs in the occupational field; economic or social factors that influence growth.

Earnings. Average earnings at various skill levels, special pay arrangements (for example, commissions), labor unions in the field, and so on. (Local pay rates may vary.)

Related Occupations. Jobs closely related to the main occupational field, suggesting alternative career choices.

Sources of Additional Information. Where to go or write for career information, training requirements, certification standards, and related information. Very important for follow-up purposes.

What did Jim learn? First of all, he found out that there were almost a million automobile mechanics! And he really didn't know what it meant to be a paid mechanic working full time in an automotive repair shop. He had been around cars ever since he was old enough to know a torque wrench from an Allen wrench, but he found that he needed a lot more information before deciding to leave the Army and put his future in the hands of a civilian employer.

What he found out from reading the *Handbook* raised doubts in his mind about his career objective. As he read the section on automobile mechanics, he took notes, underlining important points or things about which he had questions:

★ *Good employment outlook.* More job openings for auto mechanics than for most occupations. Auto repair business *not greatly affected by changing economic conditions.* During economic slumps *employers may be reluctant to hire trainees.*

★ *Army training and experience* qualifies for *entry-level trainee job. Additional on-the-job training: 3 to 5 years. Factory training needed. Trainee pay: $9.31 an hour, national average.*

★ *Good mechanics* make *quick and accurate diagnoses* of mechanical problems.

★ *Associate degree* becoming important. Courses suggested: electronics, physics, chemistry, math, and hydraulics.

★ *Service managers:* Senior mechanics who *show leadership.*

★ *Customer service reps:* mechanics who *get along well with people.*

★ Mechanics who set up independent shops need *money.*

★ *Certification* as a transmission specialist: minimum two years' experience plus written test. *Write to:* National Institute for Automotive Service Excellence, Washington, DC.

★ *Write for information about training and working conditions:* Motor and Equipment Manufacturers Association, Automotive Service Councils, Inc., Motor Vehicle Manufacturers Association of the U.S.

Jim now had a fix on the situation. He was a little upset because his Army training would only qualify him for entry-level employment, with lots of on-the-job training ahead. But the pay looked good, and he would be just 21 years old when he got out of the Army. He went through his notes point by point and listed his own qualifications:

★ High school graduate, General Diploma (not much math or science, but enjoyed what I had)

★ Two years' experience as a transmission mechanic possible by time I leave the Army

★ Good diagnostic skills

★ Good leadership and communication skills; already a team leader training new tech-school graduates

He was optimistic, and he knew he needed to do some further investigation of other options, such as: certification standards, an associate degree, and factory training.

Romancing the Objective
★★★

Now that you have established some sort of objective for civilian employment and translated your military skills into terms that civilian employers can appreciate, are you finished with planning? Of course not. You have a lot of work ahead of you to determine the course of action that will best help you accomplish your objective. How much you do and how long it will take depends on your own abilities and circumstances; one important factor is how much time you have before you leave military service. What you can do and how can, however, be set out in what might be thought of as "Standard Operating Procedures for Career Transition."

No one can tell you exactly what you should do to succeed at anything you undertake. However, one of the advantages you should have obtained from military service is knowing how to "plug into" existing guidelines, procedures, and formulas for effective action. Among other things, the military process requires dedication to the mission or objective, varying amounts of thought, the ability to identify important points while handling quantities of unorganized information, techniques for collecting additional information, willingness to adapt to changing circumstances, a sense of urgency, personal integrity, and considerable personal energy. The techniques and personal qualities needed to plug into military training guidelines or standard operating procedures can and should also be applied to developing your own civilian career transition plan. In military terms, poor planning may lead to failure to reach the objective and result in forfeiting the mission, whether it is to seize and occupy a piece of terrain or to complete an essential report on time. In civilian terms, poor planning leads to the same unacceptable results, but the difference is that it's the rest of your life that's involved. Knowing what to do, therefore, can improve the effectiveness of your transition planning. But only you can make the procedures work.

How Much Time Do You Need?

An important factor in any planning process is, of course, the time available to the planner. From the beginning, this book has encouraged you to plan ahead with some sense of urgency. How far ahead you should plan depends on your own abilities and your career objectives. Most observers of the process, however, urge that transition planning begin at least one year before your proposed or actual separation from service. In practice, that means that you should begin planning more than a year ahead of your ETS. Only in this way can you hope to take advantage of the many career transition opportunities available to you while you are still in uniform, including advanced technical training, military occupational specialty changes, and opportunities to improve your educational standing. In some cases, preliminary or provisional planning for a career transition may stretch over several years or even throughout an entire service career.

Of course, you shouldn't neglect your military duties during transition planning. Rather, the career planning tactics and strategies suggested in this book are entirely consistent with established military policies and procedures. Much of the pretransition investigation and follow-up will be done on your own time and some of it must be done off the military base. Keep in mind that the time and effort you spend on this phase of your transition planning is an investment in your future. At the same time, the information you gather and the personal contacts you make will often contribute to your effectiveness in your current or future military job or assignments.

The time factor involved in transition planning varies considerably for military personnel in different categories. No iron-clad rules apply, but the following three categories suffice for purposes of discussion.

Category A: Short-termers

Anyone who has entered military service for a tour of three to four years or less probably should have begun career planning *before* entering active duty. This applies in particular to those who enter combat arms specialties, for which there are no civilian counterparts. In general, neither enlisted personnel nor officers who enter military service for three years or less—Army enlistments can be as short as two years—can expect to acquire sufficient technical or professional skills to qualify for more than entry-level employment in the same occupational field unless they brought skills with them from civilian life. (For example, those who enlisted in programs that provided advanced training because they were already skill-qualified by military standards; commissioned health services professionals who had already earned professional degrees.) Your emphasis in transition planning should probably be on (1) improving your general educational levels while still in uniform, or (2) planning for postseparation technical or professional training to qualify for civilian employment in jobs not necessarily related to your in-service military specialty.

Many young men and women who enter military service on short-term enlistments have no postservice goals; or, if they do, their goals are vague, unrealistic, or both. If you are in Category A, you will therefore need to explore and exploit in-service avenues to postservice civilian careers as soon as possible after you enter military service.

Category B: Midterm Noncareerists

Officers and enlisted personnel who serve on active duty for five to ten years can acquire advanced technical and professional training and job skills while in uniform. Although they will age and mature during their military service, both good assets for midlevel employment, the dynamic civilian job market will move along in its own peculiar ways without them. Keeping in touch is essential. Technical and professional training obtained in earlier years, whether during or outside military service, must be updated. The civilian jobs that were "hot" when these people entered military service may have "cooled off." New career opportunities are constantly emerging.

These people should probably begin serious transition planning at least two years in advance of their ETS date, if not sooner, to be sure that they get the right kind of advanced military training, make informed changes in military occupational or officer specialty, or allow necessary time to complete an appropriate postsecondary educational program. Some experts advise people in this category to extend their service commitment, if necessary, to gain more time for completing transition planning actions.

Category C: Career-Minded Personnel

Officers and enlisted members with 11 or more years of active duty will be moving out of narrow technical specialties into the broader field of professional military development as they advance in rank. Senior noncommissioned officers (E-6 to E-9), warrant officers, and officers (O-4 and up) are generally faced with such alternatives as keeping up with original technical or professional fields; changing their transition goals to exploit their advanced training in managing people, resources, and programs; or formulating entirely new career objectives.

Men and women in this category also face the possibility of involuntary release before qualifying for retirement or of mandatory retirement as soon as they do qualify. Some are confronted with personal or family problems so severe that they can only be handled by leaving military service. No one really plans for such contingencies, but they exist. Early and continuous planning for career transition can soften the blow if it comes or improve your civilian prospects if it does not.

Category C people are those who are most apt to experience difficulty with their career transition. Career service tends to foster expectations of upper-level civilian jobs which generally go unfulfilled. Moreover, almost anyone who has been out of the civilian labor force for 20 years or more (or, more likely, has never held a significant civilian job) can expect to have lost touch with the market unless he or she has done very good transition planning over a long period of time. For everyone in this category, early and continuous contingency planning is essential. This planning will be capped by a period of intensive activity for six months to a year prior to anticipated ETS. But this is not the time to be scrambling for tactical or strategic advantage. Rather, assuming that they have planned well, this last phase can concentrate on perfecting job-search strategies and techniques needed to carry these people to a successful transition.

Case Study: *Researching the Objective*

Jim, the Army automobile mechanic we discussed earlier, did a good job of preliminary career research. The following are some additional things he did over a period of several weeks.

He talked to his supervisor and got the name of a former staff sergeant who had worked in his shop and was now working in town at an AAMCO transmission shop. The supervisor recommended that Jim visit the base education center and talk to a counselor about enrolling in a community college program. Factory training was possible in an advanced tech training program, but Jim would have to reenlist. He also wrote to all the associations listed in the *Occupational Outlook Handbook* to explain his situation and to request information.

Jim met the former staff sergeant one evening after work. They had a good talk; afterward, the older man invited Jim to visit the AAMCO shop to talk to the lead mechanic and the service manager.

Jim visited the AAMCO shop but made sure that everybody knew he was not looking for a job; he was merely seeking good advice. But he kept his eyes open as he was being shown around. Jim noticed that the shop was clean, well lighted, and airy. There was even a small lunchroom for the staff.

The service manager unexpectedly invited Jim to his home for a barbecue that weekend. At that time, he confirmed what Jim had already been hearing: He could plan on working about ten years to become a transmission rebuilder. Jim's Army training and experience would be useful, but he would only qualify as an advanced trainee. To get ahead, what he really needed was factory training, because AAMCO worked on all kinds of transmissions, American and foreign. The service manager said he liked Jim's attitude and would be glad to have him as a trainee, except that business was slow and he wasn't hiring: "Maybe in a year, after you are discharged, things will be better," he said. "Look me up then if you're still interested."

Next, Jim looked in the yellow pages and found that there were other transmission shops in town; he visited some of them to talk about what it took to become a transmission specialist. He got the same story, more or less, about a long period of on-the-job training and the need for factory training. The one thing he heard wherever he went was that business was off; nobody was hiring trainees.

He heard about another association, the Automatic Transmission Rebuilders Association, but he had no address. A friend suggested he go to the base library and ask for help. The reference librarian found the name and address for him in the *Encyclopedia of Associations*. Before he left the library, Jim learned that the association conducted advanced training sessions for mechanics who worked for its member companies. He wrote for information.

Replies to the letters he had written for information included references to books and publications that he wanted to look at. The base librarian was able to find them at the public library and borrow them through an interlibrary loan. The others were reference books, and Jim found himself driving to the public library in town several evenings. He had never visited libraries much, but the librarians were helpful and he soon felt comfortable doing his own research.

Then, Jim went home on leave for a week. His uncle introduced him to the service manager at the local Ford dealership. Not much came of this lead: Transmission work was pretty much limited to replacing damaged transmissions with new or rebuilt ones. However, the service manager sent Jim over to see Steve, the owner of the local transmission rebuild shop.

That visit was more encouraging. In the shop, he found a plaque that said the shop was a member of the Automatic Transmission Rebuilders Association. He also saw that the shop was well laid out and clean. Steve gave him hard facts: Army training and experience was helpful, but several more years of on-the-job training and some factory training would be required before he could qualify as a transmission rebuilder. Steve thought Jim might qualify as an advanced trainee, skipping over the "remove and replace" (R&R) phase (the job done by beginning trainees) right into helping rebuilders. Jim asked about the transmission rebuilders' association. Steve said that an association training team was due in that week and invited him to attend the session on an advanced Toyota transmission. Jim found that he could follow the session easily. He already knew the principles involved and quickly picked up the new points. Steve was impressed when they discussed the session afterward. As Jim left the shop, Steve gave him his business card and said, "Keep in touch, Jim. Bill, my chief rebuilder, is thinking about retiring in about a year or so. I'll be looking for someone to fill out the team."

Jim found one of his high school buddies working as a trainee mechanic in another auto repair shop. The two of them compared notes and talked shop over a pizza. Jim had to pay; his friend said he was broke until payday. "Can't hardly live alone on $4.50 an hour," he said. "Don't know when Jane and I can ever get married. You've got it made in the Army." Jim thought back to the "average wage" for trainees he had read about: $9.31 an hour. He went back to a couple of shops before leaving town and talked again to the mechanics he had met. He found that his hometown was noted for its low wages. The wives of all the mechanic trainees were out working; the more experienced mechanics were making higher wages. So, he asked himself, what else is new? Anyway, Jean was finishing up a computer program at the county college; she had already been promised a job. They were planning on having children right away.

Jim visited the education center when he returned to the base and told a counselor what he had been doing and what he had learned.

Case Study: *Starting a Business*

Mary was an E-8 who dedicated 35 years to the Army and was retiring at the age of 54. She had operated the Post Exchange for 6 years and really enjoyed this line of work. She was in a state of denial concerning retirement and anxiety concerning the job search. She had adopted JAC as her family, using all its services. She chose to stay in the area of the base due to her familiarity with the community and her network of friends.

Mary's objective was to own her own retail establishment, possibly an Army/Navy store. She was very much a self-starter, and had been careful with her financial resources throughout her military career. Her concern revolved not so much around her ability to operate a business, but more on the length of time it would take to realize a profit so she wouldn't totally deplete her savings.

Mary began her planning process by doing some research, which included the following activities:

★ Visiting and speaking with owners of similar businesses to determine their experiences, successes, and failures

★ Meeting with the local chamber of commerce to obtain demographic and psychographic data on the area

★ Establishing a relationship with an accounting firm

★ Interviewing and selecting the right legal representation

★ Interviewing and selecting a bank and banker she felt comfortable with

★ Talking with friends and family about her plans

Mary determined that she needed to live on an extremely tight budget for the first 90 days while her business was getting started; she had approximately $65,000 in savings. To establish her cash flow requirements, she filled out the forms shown in Exhibits 14.1 through 14.3. The results are summarized in the balance sheet shown in Exhibit 14.4. As this balance sheet shows, Mary needed a certain amount of cash monthly just to get the business started. This money had to come from her savings.

To determine how much time she had to make the business work, Mary used the following equation:

Available Funds ÷ Total Average Monthly Expenses (personal and business)
= Number of Months Savings Will Last

$$\$65,000 \div \$4,338 = 15 \text{ months}$$

After looking over her cash flow requirements, Mary developed her business plan and established her business as a Subchapter S corporation with her attorney's help. She felt quite confident with her decision to move forward based on solid planning.

EXHIBIT 14.1

Monthly Personal Expenses

Expenses	First Month	Second Month	Third Month
Mortgage payment	$ 750	$ 750	$ 750
House insurance premiums	$ 23	$ 23	$ 23
Property taxes	$ 180	$ 180	$ 180
Association fees	$ 110	$ 110	$ 110
Electricity/gas	$ 75	$ 75	$ 75
Water and sewage	$ 5	$ 5	$ 5
Trash collection	$ 15	$ 15	$ 15
Telephone	$ 70	$ 70	$ 70
Cable television	$ 30	$ 30	$ 30
Magazine subscriptions	$ 15	$ 15	$ 15
Household maintenance	$ 60	$ 60	$ 60
Outstanding loans	$ 0	$ 0	$ 0
Interest on loans	$ 0	$ 0	$ 0
Automobile loan payment	$ 180	$ 180	$ 180
Automobile insurance	$ 35	$ 35	$ 35
Gasoline and Oil	$ 50	$ 50	$ 50
Automobile maintenance	$ 20	$ 20	$ 20
Family expenses	$ 0	$ 0	$ 0
Personal taxes	$ 0	$ 0	$ 0
Life insurance premiums	$ 30	$ 30	$ 30
Child care	$ 0	$ 0	$ 0
Medical insurance	$ 0	$ 0	$ 0
Medical/drug expense	$ 0	$ 0	$ 0
Groceries	$ 200	$ 200	$ 200
Restaurants	$ 50	$ 50	$ 50
New clothing	$ 50	$ 50	$ 50
Laundry and dry cleaning	$ 20	$ 20	$ 20
Tuition fees	$ 0	$ 0	$ 0
Children's college fund	$ 0	$ 0	$ 0
Club membership dues	$ 0	$ 0	$ 0
Personal expenses	$ 35	$ 35	$ 35
Recreational activities	$ 0	$ 0	$ 0
Charitable contributions	$ 0	$ 0	$ 0
Emergency fund	$ 50	$ 50	$ 50
Other expenses	$ 60	$ 60	$ 60
Total Monthly Expenses	$2,113	$2,113	$2,113

EXHIBIT 14.2

Monthly Business Expenses

Expenses	First Month	Second Month	Third Month
Rental payments	$ 650	$ 650	$ 650
Insurance premiums	$ 35	$ 35	$ 35
Association fees	$ 150	$ 150	$ 150
Electricity	$ 65	$ 65	$ 65
Telephone	$ 100	$ 100	$ 100
Business loan	$ 250	$ 250	$ 250
Employee payroll	$ 0	$ 0	$ 0
Payroll taxes	$ 0	$ 0	$ 0
Accounting fees	$ 75	$ 75	$ 75
Legal fees	$ 500	$ 0	$ 0
Stationery	$ 250	$ 50	$ 50
Office supplies	$1,000	$ 50	$ 50
Advertising	$ 500	$ 500	$ 500
Total Monthly Expenses	$3,575	$1,925	$1,925

EXHIBIT 14.3
Monthly Income Revenue Streams

Revenue Stream	First Month	Second Month	Third Month
Salary	$ 0	$ 0	$ 0
Separation pay	$ 0	$ 0	$ 0
Retirement plan	$2,000	$2,000	$2,000
Unemployment	$ 0	$ 0	$ 0
Interest on savings	$ 150	$ 150	$ 150
Interest on CDs	$ 0	$ 0	$ 0
Stocks and bonds (dividends)	$ 100	$ 100	$ 100
Tax refund	$ 0	$ 0	$ 0
Debts, loans, and collection	$ 600	$ 0	$ 0
Spouse's wages	$ 0	$ 0	$ 0
Dependent's earnings	$ 0	$ 0	$ 0
Alimony	$ 0	$ 0	$ 0
Part-time/Freelance work	$ 200	$ 200	$ 200
Planned sale of property	$ 0	$ 0	$ 0
Other sources	—	—	—
Total Monthly Income	$3,050	$2,450	$2,450

EXHIBIT 14.4
Cash Flow Requirements Balance Sheet

	First Month	Second Month	Third Month
Monthly income	+$3,050	+$2,450	+$2,450
Monthly Expenses (personal)	−$2,113	−$2,113	−$2,113
Monthly Expenses (business)	−$3,575	−$1,925	−$1,925
Estimated available funds	($2,928)	($1,888)	($1,888)

Case Study: *Planning a Self-Directed Transition*

John was an Infantry O-3 who had been in the military for 12 years. During that time, his wife, Margaret, had traveled with him on each new assignment. Margaret was a self-taught, highly competent bookkeeper with excellent communication skills; however, she had only a high school diploma. John planned to leave the military in 18 months and was interested in pursuing a complete career change in the field of computers, specifically computer software.

John was 40 years old with only two years of college education. Besides obtaining employment, both John and Margaret were concerned about housing and how their lack of education could impact their chances in the marketplace. Their individual and collective objectives were as follows:

1. (John) To obtain a job as a software designer

2. (Margaret) To become a certified public accountant (CPA)

3. To purchase a new or relatively new home near their relatives

4. To complete their undergraduate studies

5. To start a family

Both John and Margaret were highly proactive. After establishing their objectives, they set up the following 18-month schedule to pave the way for a self-directed transition.

Month 1 to Month 7

1. **Assess goals.** Include personal dreams and collective ambitions, and discuss family needs (immediate family as well as extended).

2. **Identify unified objectives.**
   Answer questions such as "What kind of lifestyle do we want?" and "Where do we want to live?"

   ★ Make plans with colleges to pursue degrees.

   ★ Assemble a preliminary list of companies at which to seek employment.

3. **Organize finances and budget accordingly.**

   ★ Consult each other on eliminating or reducing expenses.

   ★ Revise portfolio and seek tax-deferred investments.

4. **Prepare resumés.**

   ★ Visit JAC for assistance.

   ★ Collect records and reports.

   ★ Complete form SF-171.

Month 7 to Month 10

1. **Review resumés.** Include a professional critique and make necessary improvements and revisions.

2. **Prepare cover letters.** Customize format and style.

3. **Research.** Look at business magazines, trade journals, national newspapers, and computer databases for industry information and employment opportunities.

4. **Establish network.** Contact friends, relatives, former associates, fellow veterans, and new contacts. Inform them of all plans and ask for assistance and support.

Month 10 to Month 13

1. **Reassess future goals.** Review all financial matters.

2. **Establish relationships.** Make contact with headhunting/recruiting firms and military associations. Send resumés to all available resources.

3. **Attend meetings.** Go to job fair interviews, self-improvement workshops, trade and industry shows, as well as all transition meetings.

4. **Continue researching.** Look further into the hidden job market; use employment newspapers.

Month 13 to Month 16

1. **Prepare for interviews.** Develop questions and answers to anticipate during the interview. Continue to refine a positive presentation.

2. **Contact employers.** Send resumés; conduct telephone follow-up.

3. **Request papers.** Get copies of separation orders, letters of recommendation, and all final performance reports.

4. **Schedule personal appointments.** Set up medical examinations, dental appointments, and quarters cleaning.

5. **Contact housing experts.** Find a mortgage company, real estate attorney, and real estate agent to help locate a new home.

6. **Coordinate move.** Arrange for all medical and insurance coverage allotment payments and the forwarding of mail and phone calls.

Month 16 to Separation

1. **Continue job search.** Maintain all contacts; send follow-up and thank-you letters to all potential employers.

2. **Complete all travel and lodging plans.** Make any vehicle repairs and farewell engagements.

3. **Purchase civilian wardrobes.**

4. **Outprocess.** Perform all property and inventory transfers and complete personnel processing.

5. **Determine budget.** Look at all transition costs (see Exhibit 14.5).

6. **Evaluate job offers.** Select employers that best suit your needs.

John and Margaret did a thorough job of planning for their transition to civilian life. Their actions were methodical, well conceived, and precisely executed. Rather than becoming overwhelmed by the enormity of the entire task, they exercised wise judgment by dividing the process into easily manageable activities.

EXHIBIT 14.5

Estimated Monthly Transition Cost

Expenses	First Month	Second Month	Third Month
Civilian clothing (suits, shirts, ties, socks, shoes, hats, gloves, belts, and accessories)	$2,000	$ 150	$ 150
Personal computer, printer, and supplies (loan)	$ 185	$ 185	$ 185
Stationery	$ 150	$ 0	$ 0
Resumé reproductions	$ 150	$ 50	$ 50
Postage	$ 100	$ 50	$ 25
Faxing and delivery fees	$ 150	$ 25	$ 25
Answering machine	$ 75	$ 0	$ 0
Long distance calls	$ 200	$ 75	$ 75
Subscription fees	$ 50	$ 50	$ 50
Gasoline	$ 100	$ 100	$ 100
Toll fees	$ 10	$ 10	$ 10
Parking fees	$ 50	$ 10	$ 10
Auto services	$ 200	$ 0	$ 0
Hotels	$ 250	$ 0	$ 0
Food	$ 200	$ 200	$ 200
Entertainment	$ 50	$ 50	$ 50
Laundry/dry cleaning	$ 30	$ 30	$ 30
Miscellaneous expenses	$ 200	$ 200	$ 200
Total Estimated Cost	$4,150	$1,185	$1,160

JOB SEARCH METHODS

★★★★★★★★★★★★★★★★★★★★★★★★★★★★★★★★★★

The following sections provide the methods you need to make your transition from the military to the civilian workplace. Using these hands-on strategies you'll be able to negotiate today's employment market and land the job you want. These are the steps to take to successfully launch your new career.

Skill Training

You have just left an organization that has the best training capabilities of any employer in the country. You might be very competitive for a similar military position, but now you need to look at the civilian environment. Given the benefits you have as a veteran, the time you may have available, and the unique nature of the civilian labor market, short- or long-term training may be your next step.

Training Opportunities
★★★

If you have moved to a medium to large city, there are many options available, five of which are as follows:

★ Company-sponsored training

★ Public night school; short-term, job-specific, one- and two-year techni-cal centers; community colleges; and universities

★ Private colleges and universities

★ Proprietary schools (one-month to two-year courses)

★ Community agencies, such as private industry councils

Each of these options has advantages and disadvantages. Time, cost, loca-tion, entrance requirements, intensity, and so on are all factors. Let's look at each option briefly.

Company-Sponsored Training

You often will hear of a company looking for skilled technicians to be trained to implement a new process or product development. The company pays for the training and offers the added benefit of employment afterward. In the fast-food industry, for example, most companies are looking and willing to pay for seasoned veterans who want to go into management. Most large companies have their own training centers and purchase additional training from the outside. The benefits are obvious; the only downside is that the training is so product specific that it is not transferable to the general labor market. Thus, you need to be sure that you want to invest your career in this specific company before spending your time learning its technology.

Public Schools, Institutions, and Colleges

In most or all states, you have a blend of institutions that match the state's labor market demand. The problem could be that the training you want and need may not be available in your city.

Most public schools, including high schools, offer short-term, skill- or job-specific training. If you only read to brush up on a skill, this is by far the cheapest investment of time and money. Most schools can provide credentials of competence that are recognized by unions and employers.

One- to two-year technical institutes and community colleges demand more of your time. Although you can take refresher courses at night, most people enroll for a specific license, certificate, or associate degree. To shorten the time required, you may be able to test out of many courses because of your previous experience and training.

At public universities, the process is basically the same, but you obtain more advanced credentials. Again, most colleges and universities will allow you to test out of numerous standard courses, so you may not need to fulfill the full four years.

Along with your veterans' benefits, there are also grants, loans, and scholarships available to help pay for your schooling.

Private Colleges and Universities

These institutions are usually small, very expensive, and either very general (liberal arts) or very specific (engineering). The best of the best demand the best, so entrance requirements are tough. One nice feature, if you are eligible, could be a range of private scholarships to help offset the high cost. Check out schools' reputations closely; if they're accredited you're normally all right.

Proprietary Schools

There is a proprietary school or college for almost every occupational specialty. Proprietary schools are for profit and normally don't carry as much clout with employers as two-year institutions. One benefit is that courses of study are quick. Because you are targeting a specific job, not a career field, these schools can prepare you in a matter of months. They also have a wide range of scholarships available, many of which go unclaimed each year.

Community Agencies

There are usually a number of public community agencies commissioned to train and retrain people in jobs specific to the community labor market. Private industry councils, for example, have federal funds to test, counsel, enroll, certify, and place young people and adults. They have financing for transportation, child care, tuition, food, and fees; are well connected in each community, and have very acceptable placement rates.

Selecting a Program

The terrain is fairly easy to navigate. First, if you simply want to study all training facilities' information, you can get directories, microfiche, or computer programs at your public library, employment services, community college, and high school. Go to your local high school counselor, who should have current data on schools in various formats. He or she also should be a little more objective in evaluating institutions because he or she has nothing to gain by your enrollment.

Next, make an appointment to visit prospective schools. Take a tour, talk to instructors, chat with the students, and check out placement offices and services.

For more specific information on college selection, refer to Chapter 8.

Scheduling Your Time

We often feel uneasy, unwanted, discouraged, disengaged, and sometimes lost and disappointed about being separated from one job and just waiting for prospective employers to call. We tend to want to rush the job hunt because it is unnatural to be unemployed. Your original career goal has been interrupted or ended due to an unexpected (or even expected) layoff or early retirement.

You need to schedule wisely; take time and prepare for reentry. We often jump at the first opportunity, only to be disappointed when a better job becomes available a week or a month later. Like getting married, purchasing a home, or selecting a college, you need to take time to be sure about your choice.

You have options to buy yourself some time if the market isn't ready. Unemployment compensation is a resource, not an embarrassment. It can give you time to conduct a thorough search, create a winning set of credentials, and do some retraining to tailor your military experience to the civilian labor market. You need to study your resources fully and determine what investments you need to make to prepare yourself to be an ideal job candidate.

During any major transition, you need time to do the following:

★ *Compare* local job opportunities

★ *Observe* the current and pending labor markets

★ *Initiate* a complete and professional job hunt

★ *Arrange* meetings, company visits, and transition assistance

★ *Research* work options, such as self-employment, part-time work, and companies coming to town

★ *Plan* a job hunt like a new business plan

★ *Organize* a powerful set of credentials/portfolio

★ *Motivate* yourself by being around positive people and activities

★ *Budget* to make sure you have the money to buy the time you need

★ *Listen* and tune in to the job market information network

★ *Promote* yourself

The issue of time is not so much how much you put into the job hunt, but how you use your time. You need to stay alert and always be ready for a call. Combining relaxation and exercise during your job search is critical. It is possible to be so ready you go blank or fall asleep at the interview.

Unemployment has or can drain you physically and psychologically. For some people, dealing with these effects are more important than one more phone call or one more letter. Balance is the answer, but you must plan for balance. Plan your job reentry in the same way you were taught to plan for work. The form on page 189 will give you some ideas on how to prepare a strategic plan for reemployment. The variables for planning are as follows:

★ Letter writing

★ Corporate researching

★ Personal networking

★ Attending meetings

★ Interviewing

★ Credential building

★ Conducting mock interviews

★ Resumé writing

★ Developing lead lists

★ Taking time for recreation

★ Ensuring family health and welfare

★ Taking time for physical activity

★ Filling out applications

Planning for Reemployment.

Day	Date	Time	General Activity	Tasks to be Performed	Expectations
Wed.	6/27/94	8:00 A.M.	Visit with church secretary	1. Locate church directory 2. Make log of key persons and data	Ten parish members who own or operate a business

Resumés and Application Forms

You might see a hurdle to leap over, a hoop to jump through, or a barrier to knock down. That is how many people think of resumés, cover letters, interviews, and application forms. But you don't have to think of them that way. They are not ways to keep you from a job; they are ways for you to show an employer what you know and what you can do. After all, you're going to get a job; it's just a question of which one.

Employers want to hire people who can do the job. To learn who these people are, they use resumés, application forms, written tests, performance tests, medical examinations, and interviews. You can use each of these different evaluation procedures to your advantage.

Effective Resumés and Application Forms
★★

Resumés and application forms are two ways to achieve the same goal: Give the employer written evidence of your qualifications. When creating a resumé or completing an application form, you need two different kinds of information: Facts about yourself and facts about the job you want. With this information in hand, you can present the facts about yourself in terms of the available job. You have more freedom with a resumé—you can put your best points first and avoid weak spots. But, even on application forms, you can describe your qualifications in terms of the job's duties.

Resumés: Your Introduction to an Employer
★★

A resumé is a brief sketch of your background which provides an employer with a summary of your education, work experience, special skills, and training.

In a successful job hunt, you must draw the employers attention to you and separate yourself from the other job applicants. A most effective way to do this is with a well-written resumé.

Purpose of Resumés

The main purpose of a resumé is to make an employer interested in learning more about you. Everyone can and should use a resumé to make their qualifications known to potential employers. The job candidate whose resumé reaches the largest number of employers has the greatest chance of success in obtaining job interviews. Because you will only be hired after a satisfactory interview, you must concentrate your energies on securing as many interviews as possible. Your resumé (and accompanying cover letter when needed) is the single most effective tool at your disposal to get an employer's attention and make him or her want to talk to you.

It is your job to identify as many potential employers as possible and get your resumé into their hands. Most people send resumés only in response to advertised positions; however, there are a number of other ways to get your resumé on the desk of a prospective employer. When filling out job applications, make yourself stand out by attaching a copy of your resumé to the application. When you mention your job search to friends or neighbors, give them copies of your resumé to pass on to their business associates who may be able to offer you some guidance in your job-hunting efforts. When you identify a potential employer, send him or her a resumé along with a cover letter expressing your interest in the company.

You will only obtain a position you desire by meeting employers face to face and helping them see you as the person they want and need. Your resumé may be your first or last contact with them, so you have to make it good!

Creating a Winning Resumé

All resumés are designed to do the same thing: Tell prospective employers something about the job-seeker. No matter how they are set up and regardless of the information included on them, all resumés try to encourage an employer to call the sender for an interview. In many cases, the majority of job applicants will not use a resumé and cover letter; the mere fact that you have a good-looking resumé is likely to get you in the door for an interview. (An employer is likely to think that if only 1 in 25 applicants has a resumé, that one is likely to be the person he or she wants to talk to about the job.) In other cases, where almost all of the competing job candidates use resumés, those applications who've taken the time to think about how they present themselves to prospective employers will fare better than those who simply present their information in a disorganized and unfocused manner.

The following are suggestions to help you develop the information you will want to present to an employer. While there are no hard and fast rules about what the format should look like, most resumés present similar types of information. Choose those most descriptive of the kind of employee and person you see yourself to be.

★ **Know thyself.** Begin by assembling information about yourself. Use the exercises you completed in Chapter 6. Some items appear on virtually every resumé, including the following:

—Current address and phone number. If you are rarely at home during business hours, try to give the phone number of a friend or relative who will take messages for you.

—The job you want or your career goal.

—Experience (paid and volunteer). Include dates of employment, name and full address of the employer, job title, starting and finishing salaries, and reason for leaving (moving, returning to school, and seeking a better position are among the readily accepted reasons).

—Education. Include the school's name, the city in which it is located, the years you attended, the diploma or certificate you earned, and the course of studies you pursued.

—Other qualifications. List any relevant hobbies, organizations to which you belong, honors you have received, and leadership positions you have held.

—Office machines, tools, and equipment you have used and special skills that you possess.

★ **Know thy job.** Next, gather specific information about the jobs you are applying for. You should already have this information from the research you did in Chapter 11. You need to know the pay range (so you can make their top figure your bottom price), the education and experience usually required, and the hours and shifts usually worked. Most importantly, you need to know the job duties (so that you can describe your experience in terms of those duties). Study the job description. Some job announcements, especially those issued by the government, even have a checklist that assigns a numerical weight to different qualifications so you can be certain which is the most important. Looking at such announcements will give you an idea of what employers look for even if you do not wish to apply for a government job. If the announcement or ad is vague, call the employer to learn what he or she is looking for.

Once you have the information you need, you can prepare a resumé. You may need to prepare more than one master resumé if you are going to look for different kinds of jobs. Otherwise, your resumé will not be tailored correctly to each job's requirements.

Two Kinds of Resumés

The way you arrange your resumé depends on how well your experience has prepared you for the position you want. Basically, you can either describe your most recent job first and work backwards (chronological resumé) or group similar skills together (functional resumé). No matter which format you use, the following advice applies generally.

- ★ Use specifics. A vague description of your duties will make only a vague impression.

- ★ Identify your accomplishments. If you headed a project, improved productivity, reduced costs, increased membership, or achieved some other goal, say so.

- ★ Type your resumé using a standard typeface. Printed resumes are becoming more common, but employers do not indicate a preference for them.

- ★ Keep the length down to one page, two at most.

- ★ Remember your mother's advice to not say anything if you cannot say something nice. Leave all embarrassing or negative information off the resumé, but be ready to deal with it in a positive manner at the interview.

- ★ Proofread the master copy carefully.

- ★ Have someone else proofread the master copy carefully.

- ★ Have a third person proofread the master copy carefully.

- ★ Use the best-quality photocopying machine and good white or off-white paper.

- ★ Send written references only if the employer requests them.

- ★ Do not date your resumé.

- ★ Do not use abbreviations that are not commonly understood.

- ★ If an employer asks for your salary requirements, put them in your cover letter, never on your resumé.

- ★ Do not attach a photo or classified ad to your resumé.

Example of a Chronological Resumé

Allison Springs
15 Hilton House
College de l'Art Libre
Smallville, CO 77717

(666) 555-3550

JOB SOUGHT: Hotel Management Trainee

EDUCATION:

September 1983 to June 1987	College de l'Art Libre College Lane Smallville, CO 77717	Vice President, Junior Class (raised $15,000 for junior project) Member, College Service Club (2 years) Swim Team (4 years) Harvest Celebration Director Major: Political Science with courses in economics and accounting
July 1987 to June 1988	U.S. Army Dantes Training Program	Certification: Administrative Services

EXPERIENCE:

Period employed	Employer	Job title and duties
June 1987–present	U.S. Army Supervisor: Col. John Myers	Various positions in Personnel, Department of U.S. Army, Assession Division
January 1987–present 10 hours per week	McCall, McCrow, and McCow 980 Main Street Westrow, CO 77718 Supervisor: Jan Eagelli	Research assistant: Conducted research on legal and other matters for members of the firm.
September 1986– December 1986 10 hours per week	Department of Public Assistance State of Colorado 226 Park Street Smallville, CO 77717 Supervisor: James Fish	Claims interviewer: Interviewed clients to determine their eligibility for various assistance programs. Directed them to special administrators when appropriate.
Summers, 1980–1985	Shilo Pool 46 Waterway Shilo, NE 77777	Lifeguard: Insured safety of patrons by seeing that rules were obeyed, testing chemical content of the water, and inspecting mechanical equipment.

References/reommendations available upon request.

Example of a Functional Resumé

Allison Springs
15 Hilton House
College de l'Art Libre
Smallville, CO 77717

(666) 555-3550

JOB SOUGHT: Hotel Management Trainee

SKILLS, EDUCATION, AND EXPERIENCE:

Working with people: All the jobs I have had involve working closely with a large variety of people on many different levels. As Vice President of the Junior Class, I balanced the concerns of different groups in order to reach a common goal. As a claims interviewer with a state public assistance agency, I dealt with people under very trying circumstances. As a research assistant with a law firm, I worked with both lawyers and clerical workers, and as a lifeguard (five summers), I learned how to manage groups of people.

Effective communication: My campaign for class office, committee projects, and fund-raising efforts (which netted $15,000 for the junior class project), relied on effective commuication in both oral and written presentations.

Organization and management: My participation in the U.S. Army Personnel Department has developed my organizational and management skills. In addition, my work with the state government and a law office has made me familiar with organizational procedures.

CHRONOLOGY:

1980 to 1985	Worked as lifeguard during the summers at the Shilo Pool, 46 Waterway, Shilo, Nebraska 77777
September 1983 to June 1987	Attended College de l'Art Libre in Smallville, Colorado. Earned a Bachelor of Arts degree in political science. Elected Vice President of the Junior Class, managed successful fund drive, directed Harvest Celebration Committee, served on many other committees, and earned 33 percent of college expenses.
September 1986 to December 1986	Worked as claims interviewer intern for the Department of Public Assistance for the State of Colorado, 226 Park Street, Smallville, Colorado 77717. Supervisor: James Fish
January 1987 to present	Work as research assistant for the law office of McCall, McCrow, and McCow, 980 Main Street, Westrow, Colorado 77718. Supervisor: Jan Eagelli
June 1987 to present	U.S. Army Administrative Assistant in Personnel, U.S. Army Assession Division Supervisor: Col. John Myers

Recommendations available on request.

Reverse chronology is the easier method to use. It is also the least effective because it makes when you did something more important than what you did. It is an especially poor format if you have gaps in your work history, if the job you seek is very different from the job you currently hold, or if you are entering the civilian job market for the first time. About the only time you want to use such a resumé is when you have progressed up a clearly defined career ladder and want to move up a rung. An example of a chronological resumé is shown on page 194.

Resumés that are not chronological may be called functional, analytical, skill oriented, creative, or something else. The differences are less important than the similarity, which is that all of them stress what you can do. The advantage to a potential employer—and, therefore, to your job campaign—should be obvious. The employer can see immediately how you will fit the job. This format also has advantages because it camouflages gaps in your employment or the fact that you have only had one employer.

You begin writing a functional resumé by determining the skills the employer is looking for. Again, study the job description for this information. Next, review your experience and education to see when you demonstrated the abilities sought. Then, prepare the resume itself, putting the information that relates most obviously to the job first. The result will be a resumé with headings such as, Engineering, Computer Languages, Communications Skills, or Design Experience. These headings will have much more impact than the dates you would use on a chronological resumé. An example of a functional resumé is given on page 195.

It is much easier to make a bad impression than a good one. Treat your resumé as though it is the only contact you will have with an employer and that it is the deciding factor in your obtaining an interview and a job. If you don't, your resumé probably *will be* the only contact you will have with the employer.

Application Forms

★★★

Some large employers, such as fast-food franchises and government agencies, use application forms more than resumés. The forms suit the style of large organizations because people can find information more quickly if it always appears in the same place. However, creating a resumé before filling out an application form will still help you. Application forms are really just resumés in disguise. No matter how rigid the form appears to be, you can still use it to show why you are the person for the job being filled.

At first glance, application forms seem to give a job hunter no leeway. The forms certainly do not have the flexibility of a resumé, but you can still use them to your best advantage. Remember that the attitude of the person reading the form is not, "Let's find out why this person is unqualified," but, "Maybe this is the person we want." Use all the parts of the form—experience blocks, education blocks, and others—to show that that person is you.

Here's some general advice on completing application forms:

★ Request two copies of the form. If only one is provided, photocopy it before you make a mark on it. You'll need more than one copy to prepare rough drafts.

★ Read the whole form before you begin.

★ Prepare a master copy if the same form is used by several divisions within the same company or organization. Do not put the specific job applied for, date, and signature on the master copy; fill in that information on the photocopies as you submit them.

★ Type the form, if possible. If there are lots of little lines, type the information on a piece of blank paper that will fit in the overall space, paste the paper on the form, and photocopy the finished product. Such a procedure results in a neater, easier-to-read page.

★ Leave no blanks; enter "N/A" (for not applicable) when the information requested does not apply to you. This tells people checking the form that you did not simply skip a question.

★ Carry a resumé and a copy of other frequently requested information (such as previous addresses) with you when visiting potential employers in case you must fill out an application on the spot. Whenever possible, however, fill the form out at home and mail it in with a resumé and a cover letter that highlight your strengths.

Providing Information

The information from Chapter 6 that you used to create your resumé is also applicable to the job application. Check the following list to be sure you have all necessary information. Anything not included in your resumé should be listed on a separate sheet of paper. Take this paper with you when you meet potential employers in case you need to fill out an application form.

★ Your Social Security number.

★ Your current address, including city, state, zip code, county, and township. Record how long you have lived at this address.

★ Telephone numbers where you can be reached, including the area code.

★ Names and addresses of schools and training programs you have attended, the dates you attended, your courses of study, grades completed, and diplomas or certification given. If you received a GED, list the date it was received. Also list the school, military program, or institution from which you received it.

★ Names of past employers and the dates of employment. (Also list a current employer if you are now working part-time.) Highlight the diversified jobs you held while in the military, but only those that apply.

★ Responsibilities you have had in each job.

★ Equipment you have used and any related training you received.

★ Volunteer jobs. List these in the same way you would list paid work experience. Put down your position, the hours you worked, the dates you worked, your responsibilities, equipment you used, and any training you received.

★ Your skills. List those you brought to each job and others you acquired on the job.

★ Names, addresses, telephone numbers, and the company affiliations of your references.

Answer Questions Positively

Give positive reasons for leaving a previous job. Do not give negative responses, such as the following:

★ The employer didn't like me.

★ I didn't think the pay was high enough.

★ I didn't like the other workers.

★ I was injured on the job.

★ I was fired.

★ I was bored with the work.

Instead, use the following kinds of positive responses:

★ I wanted a job with more responsibility.

★ I wanted a job with more opportunities for advancement.

★ I became a full-time student.

★ I became interested in another type of work.

★ I started by own business.

★ The military was downsizing.

Don't consider common ailments when answering questions about health. Most people have colds, flu, aches, and pains sometime in life. Employers want to know if you can do the job. Write that your health is excellent if you have nothing seriously wrong with you.

List Good References

Choose former employers, teachers, and businesspeople who know you and who will say good things about you. Don't list relatives unless absolutely necessary. Choose people who can be easily contacted because employers may need to act quickly. Ask the people you want to list as references if you may do so. Tell them when they might expect calls from employers.

Read the Instructions Carefully

Watch for the words, "Do not write in this space." Make sure you follow the directions. Ask questions if you do not understand an instruction.

Write in a Neat, Legible Manner

Erase carefully. If you are filling the application out at the company, print if directed to do so or if your handwriting is poor. If you make a mistake and cannot correct it neatly, ask for a second application.

Spell Correctly

Find out how to spell words you will need to use before you go to apply for the job. Make sure you know the spelling of technical terms related to the job you are seeking. If you are unsure of a spelling when you are in the employer's office, use a word you know how to spell.

Be Honest But Don't Volunteer Too Much Information

Do not mention disabilities on the application, unless the disability could interfere with your ability to do the job. However, you can and should mention any disabilities in the interview.

If you have a criminal conviction, you can do the following:

★ Leave the space blank if the crime was minor. This information is hard for employers to get. It must be released by you.

★ Leave the space blank if you have been convicted of a felony (major crime). Discuss the topic in the interview. If the application states that you must mention the conviction, do so.

Review Your Completed Application

Make sure the information you have recorded is accurate.

Practice Makes Perfect

The following pages provide a completed sample job application which was developed from several commonly used employment application forms. By matching your personal information to the form provided, you will be better prepared to fill out the forms you may encounter in your job search.

Sample Application Form

P E R S O N A L	Last Name First Middle **(1)** Roberts John Michael	Today's Date **(2)** 1/28/94
	Present Address 200 Webster Road	Home Phone 666/555-2783
	City, State, Zip Boston, MA 02115	How long there? **(3)** 4 years
	Previous Address 565 Hillside Court	Social Security No. **(4)** 123-45-6789
	City, State, Zip Boston, MA 02117	How long there? 5 years

J O B I N F O R M A T I O N	Position Applied for **(5)** Bindery/Finishing	Full-time Part-time **(6)**	Pay Expected **(7)** $8.00/hour
	Have you ever worked for us before? If yes, when and where? **(8)** No		Date available for work **(9)** 2 weeks notice
	Hours available for work **(10)** 7-7 Mon.-Sat.	Will you work overtime, if asked? **(11)** Yes	How were you referred to us? **(12)** Patriot News
	Can you travel if position requires it? **(13)** Yes		Do you have a valid driver's license? **(14)** Yes, auto
	Are you between the ages of 18–70? If not, please state your age. **(15)** Yes		
	Are you legally eligible for employment in the United States. **(16)** Yes		
	Do you have any physical condition which may limit your ability to perform the job applied for? If yes, describe. **(17)** No		
	Person to notify in case of an emergency Relationship Phone **(18)** Helen Roberts Mother 666/555-2783		

School		Name and Location	Years Attended	Did you graduate?	Subjects Studied
E D U C A T I O N	College	**(19)** **(20)**	**(21)**	**(22)**	**(23)**
	High School	Boston High School **(24)** Boston, MA	4	Yes	Business
	Other (specify)	Boston Tech Institute **(25)** Boston, MA	1	N/A	Printing (evening class)

continued

List any memberships in professional or civic organizations. (Exclude those which may indicate your race, creed, or national origin.)
Eagle Scouts, Assistant Leader   **(26)**

List any interests or hobbies.
Hiking, restoring old cars.   **(27)**

EMPLOYMENT	Begin with the most recent position. Include military service assignments and volunteer activities.

	Company Name **(28)** Prime Print	Phone **(29)** 666/555-6798
1	Address **(30)** 75 Commerical Street Cambridge, MA	Employed (month/year) from to **(31)** 6/92 1/94
	Name of Supervisor (32) William Bennett	Weekly/Hourly Pay Start Last **(33)** $260/week $290/week
	Job Title Duties **(34)** Bindery Apprentice **(35)** AB Dick Collator Finishing	Reason for Leaving Need opportunity **(36)**

	Company Name Upton Grocery	Phone 666/555-7892
2	Address 543 Kingston Avenue Cambridge, MA	Employed (month/year) from to 12/91 6/92
	Name of Supervisor Mary Ann Kowalcik	Weekly/Hourly Pay Start Last $4.75/hour $5.25/hour
	Job Title Duties Stock clerk Stock shelves	Reason for Leaving Job advancement

	Company Name Jack's Sub Shop	Phone 666/555-1411
3	Address 67 Granite Street Cambridge, MA	Employed (month/year) from to 8/91 12/91
	Name of Supervisior Jack Sanchez	Weekly/Hourly Pay Start Last $4/hour $4.25/hour
	Job Title Duties Counter-help Make sandwiches	Reason for Leaving Needed more hours

continued

(37) We may contact the employers listed above unless you indicate those you do not want us to contact.	DO NOT CONTACT Employer Number(s) _____ Reason _____

(38)	**REFERENCES**	List below the names of three persons, not related to you, whom you have known at least one year.		
Name Address	Mike Hardy 58 Elm, Milton	Position **(39)** Teacher	Phone **(40)** 777/555-2343	Years Known **(41)** 3 years
Name Address	Barbara Houle 235 Webster, Boston	Position Neighbor	Phone 666/555-6891	Years Known 4 years
Name Address	Jim Fox 211 Tremont, Boston	Position Scout Leader	Phone 666/555-4586	Years Known 6 years

So you can avoid making some common mistakes, the following is a detailed explanation of those items in the sample application form that have proven most troublesome to job applicants:

Item 1: Applications vary, so be aware of the name (first/last) order they request.

Item 2: If you have to ask a personnel officer the day's date, you will unwittingly be making a comment about your organizational skills. Check the calendar before you leave the house for the day.

Item 3: How long you have lived at a particular residence gives an employer some sense for how long you are likely to remain in the area. All employers like consistency on the job site, and job turnover is definitely an issue for many employers. They will take into account your varied residences caused by military job location movement.

Item 4: Have this with you, all job applications require it.

Item 5: Be specific. You should know enough about the company to know whether the position you want is one the company offers. If you are responding to a newspaper advertisement, use the same job title the employer used.

Item 6: Full-time means 35 hours a week or more.

Item 7: Be realistic; many entry-level positions only pay minimum wage. The more experience and job skills you have, the better the salary you can expect to command.

   If you are uncertain as to what salary the employer may be offering or where you might fall if there is a range being offered, you may write "open" in order to leave room for negotiation.

Item 8: Past job performance is often a good indication of future job performance. The likelihood of your being hired is improved if you have had successful military and civilian work experience.

Item 9: If there is some reason you will not be available immediately, give a specific date or time period after which you will be available.

   If you are planning on taking vacation after you leave service, give the actual date you will be available upon your return.

Item 10: If you are not available for work on weekends or on certain evenings, you need to make it clear what hours and days you are available for work.

Item 11: Be honest, but remember that some employers place a high priority on acquiring employees who are very flexible in the amount of time they are willing to work.

Item 12: Specify newspaper, employment agency, employee of firm, friend, or other contact. The name of an individual can be important to both you and your prospective employer, since he or she will most likely check with that individual to find out about you and your employment history.

Item 13: Certain types of work require you to travel to different job sites from day to day or week to week. Distances can sometimes be as great as 50 miles or more, and employers do not always reimburse employees for that expense. If there are limits past which you prefer not to go, identify them (for example, 25-mile travel radius, not more than three days a week).

Item 14: If your answer is "yes," you should also provide details on what kind of license(s) you have (auto, chauffeur, bus, semi-trailer, and so forth)

Item 15: The federal Age Discrimination Act prohibits discrimination on the basis of age with respect to individuals who are at least 40 but less than 70 years of age.

Item 16: Employers may be prosecuted if they knowingly hire illegal workers. Proof of citizenship (such as a birth certificate or separation papers from the Armed Forces) or documents from the U.S. Immigration and Naturalization Service may be required.

Item 17: Physical disabilities can only be taken into consideration if they would prevent you from adequately performing a particular job. Therefore, being confined to a wheelchair does not fall into that category if you seek work as a computer programmer (physical mobility is not a part of the job description). It does fall into that category if the work requires physical exertion, such as that required of a firefighter. List only those disabilities that would have an impact on your ability to do the job for which you are applying.

Item 18: Give a person's name who knows you well and can be contacted during working hours.

Item 19: Include any continuing education classes you have taken to improve your job performance or satisfy licensing requirements.

Items 20 and 24: If you attended more than one, give the last one.

Item 21: 1 = freshman; 4 = senior. If you graduated, use 4. If you left school prior to graduation, give the last *full* year you completed. For example, if you left during your senior year, you would list 3. If you have a high school equivalency certificate, write 4 for high school completed.

Item 22: As with any other question, if the question doesn't apply to you, put "N/A" (not applicable). If you didn't graduate, use N/A.

Item 23: If your subjects of study included something of particular interest to a prospective employer for this particular job, list it here.

Item 25: List any special courses you have taken, any seminars or workshops you've attended, and any conference in which you participated. This is also where you list any college work beyond a four-year degree.

Items 26 and 27: What do you do with your spare time? Do you belong to any organizations that either demonstrate overall maturity and responsibility, or an interest or talent that may be job-related?

Item 28: Be sure to list your most recent job first.

Item 29: If he or she is interested in you, an employer will undoubtedly want to talk to the people for whom you have worked previously. Make sure you provide the correct phone numbers.

Item 30: Make sure the information you provide is accurate. Use the phone book if you are unsure as to correct street numbers.

Item 31: Do not list jobs that lasted for less than three months.

Item 32: Use the name of the person who oversaw your day-to-day activities.

Item 33: Increases in salary are a good indication that previous employers thought you were doing good work and wanted to keep you around.

Item 34: Be as specific as possible.

Item 35: Provide as much detail as space will allow. Make sure to include any responsibilities or duties that have a direct bearing on the job for which you are applying.

Item 36: Be honest, but do not provide a long list that belittles coworkers or previous employers.

Item 37: If you are presently employed, it may be advisable to keep your job hunting in confidence so as not to upset a working relationship with your colleagues or employer. Except for this situation, any answer other than "none" raises doubts about your ability to work for and with others.

Item 38: When giving references, do not provide the names of any close family relatives or the names of employers you have previously listed in your employment history. Your references should be able to speak favorably about your character, reliability, and responsibility.

Item 39: In what capacity do you know this person? How well do you know him or her? What is his or her job title?

Item 40: Here, again, do not make a prospective employer do the legwork you should have done. If you do not provide accurate information on your application, an employer may quickly decide you are not worth the additional time and trouble.

Item 41: The longer you have known someone, the greater weight his or her opinion will carry.

The application sample and directions were taken from the booklet titled, "The Application," developed by the School District of Philadelphia, published by the Life Skills Education Corporation, 314 Washington Street, Northfield, MN 55057. You may find their booklet on job applications, interviews, cover letters, and so on very valuable.

Cover Letters

You will need a cover letter whenever you send a resumé or application form to a potential employer. The letter should capture the employer's attention, show why you are writing, indicate how your skills will benefit the company, and ask for an interview. The specificity of information that must be included in a letter means that each must be written individually. Each letter must also be typed perfectly; word processing equipment helps. Frequently only the address, first paragraph, and specifics concerning an interview will vary. These items are easily changed on computers, word processors, and memory typewriters. If you do not have access to such equipment, you might be able to rent it or have your letters typed by a resumé or employment services company listed in the yellow pages. Be sure you know the full cost of such a service before agreeing to use it.

Let's examine the structure of the cover letter point by point using the sample on page 210.

★ **Salutation.** Each letter should be addressed by name to the person with whom you want to speak. That person is the one who can hire you. This is almost certainly not someone in the personnel department, and it is probably not a department head either. It is most likely to be the person who will actually supervise you once you start work. Call the company to make sure you have the right name and spell it correctly.

★ **Opening.** The opening should appeal to the reader. Cover letters are sales letters. Sales are made after you capture a person's attention. You capture the reader's attention most easily by talking about the company rather than yourself. Mention projects under development at, recent awards to, or favorable comments published about the company. You can find such information in the business press, including the business section of local newspapers and the many magazines that are devoted to particular industries. If you are answering an ad, you may mention it. If someone suggested that you write, use his or her name (with permission, of course).

★ **Body.** The body of the letter gives a brief description of your qualifications and refers to the (enclosed) resumé, where your sales campaign can continue.

★ **Closing.** You cannot have what you don't ask for. At the end of the letter, request an interview. Suggest a time and state that you will confirm the appointment. Use a standard complimentary closing, such as, "Sincerely yours," leave three or four lines for your signature; and type your name. Type your phone number under your name. The alternative is to place the phone number in the body of the letter where it will be more difficult to find should the reader wish to call you.

Example of a Cover Letter

15 Hilton House
College de l'Art Libre
Smallville, CO 77717

March 18, 1994

Ms. Collette Recruiter
Rest Easy Hotels
1500 Suite Street
Megapolis, SD 99999

Dear Ms. Recruiter:

The Rest Easy Hotels always served as a landmark for me when I traveled through this country and Europe. I would like to contribute to their growth, especially their new chain, the Suite Rest Hotels, that feature reception rooms for every guest. I have had many jobs working with people and have always enjoyed this aspect of my experience. Knowing its importance to your company, I believe I would be an asset to the Rest Easy Hotels.

During the week of March 31, I will be visiting Megapolis and would like to speak with you concerning your training program for hotel managers. I will call your secretary to confirm an appointment.

The enclosed resume outlines my education and experience.

Sincerely yours,

Allison Springs
(666) 555-3550

Remember, the cover letter to an application or request for an interview is your first introduction to someone you want to meet. In summary, it serves five purposes:

1. To introduce you to a potential employer.

2. To tell the reader a little about you.

3. To show your writing and thinking skills.

4. To show insights into your personality.

5. To provide the first clue as to the likelihood of your fit with the company, and the job available.

The letter should not rehash your resumé. Let the resumé deal with specifics. You want to excite an employer's interest so that he or she will take time to study your credentials fully.

Types of Cover Letters
★★

There are three types of cover letters and, although each transmits your credentials, they are designed to do something different. Knowing to whom you are writing and why will help you select the correct one.

★ **Response cover letter.** The company has announced a position(s) and gives clues as to how to apply.

★ **Blind cover letter.** You are not sure if a specific company has positions open, but you'd like to work there and you at least want to register your credentials and interests for future reference.

★ **Request for assistance.** These are used when you're still surveying the field and you need some inside help on identifying opportunities. First, attempt to get names of key "insider" people within a company and write to them for assistance. This process is covered in more detail in Chapter 13.

The Right Approach
★★

The following are some points to keep in mind as you send out letters and resumés:

★ Use 8½" × 11" paper, in the same texture and color as your resumé.

★ Use the same typeface for everything. Your letter and resumé are reflections of who you are.

★ Proofread, edit, edit, and proofread again.

★ Date and sign all letters.

★ Be brief (one page), but be positive and focused.

★ Use only businesslike writing conventions.

★ Don't use fancy, cute greetings or first names.

★ Don't focus on salary, fringe benefits, vacations, and so on.

★ Try not to appear to be pushy.

For Further Reading

Martin, Eric, and Karyn Langhorne. *Cover Letters They Don't Forget*. Lincolnwood, IL: VGM Career Horizons, 1993.

Portfolios

A personal portfolio contains evidence of your credentials for employment. Simply, it's an organizer that prepares you, in advance, for any questions, requirements, or requests an employer may have. It needs to be a full representation of who you are, where you've been, what you've achieved, where you'd like to be, and what work you're most interested in and qualified for. Many of the other chapters and sections of this book discuss how you might prepare and use what would be in your portfolio.

Another way of looking at the value and use of a personal portfolio is to hypothesize that an employer doesn't have time to interview you at the present time and requests a representative set of information to study before making a decision to interview you. In this case, you'd need to project what would be important to a personnel manager and what evidence he or she would be looking for. You'd then need to package all the answers in a logical, readable, and believable fashion:

★ Logical, in that your credentials flow in the order of importance for the reader

★ Readable, in the context that it's typed, clear, and complete enough to understand your credentials

★ Believable refers to having sufficient objective data (letters of support, certification documents) to back up your credentials statements

The following pages show a suggested format and content checklist for your employment credentials packet (portfolio).

Checklist of Portfolio Contents

☐ Resumé   ☐ Certificates earned

☐ Sample completed job application ☐ Letters of recommendation

☐ References   ☐ Competency exam results

☐ Diplomas/degrees   ☐ Special awards

☐ Career planner   ☐ Union documentation

☐ COPP Materials   ☐ Military papers

☐ Work-related licenses   ☐ Other _____

☐ Career interest searches   ☐ _____

☐ Standardized test scores   ☐ _____

☐ Previous employment credentials ☐ _____

Inside Front Cover of Portfolio

OCCUPATIONAL PREFERENCES
Specific Job Interest _____

Apprenticeship Experience _____

EDUCATIONAL EXPERIENCE
School _____

Years attended _____
Diploma/Degree _____
Year completed _____
Major _____

School _____

Years attended _____
Diploma/Degree _____
Year completed _____
Major _____

Military Training
Specialty _____
Years attended _____
Diploma/Degree _____
Year completed _____
Major _____

LEISURE ACTIVITIES _____

TEST SCORES (Interest, Aptitude, Achievement, ACT, SAT, Personality) (Note: Provide actual documentation in portfolio.)

Test _____ Score _____

WORK EXPERIENCE (most recent first)
Company Name _____

Supervisor's name _____

Dates employed _____
Duties _____

Company Name _____

Supervisor's name _____

Dates employed _____
Duties _____

Company Name _____

Supervisor's name _____

Dates employed _____
Duties _____

Company Name _____

Supervisor's name _____

Dates employed _____
Duties _____

Inside Back Cover

Ideal Education and Training Plan **This Year**	**Work/Job/Career Plan** **This Year (Job/Work)**
1. Competency Area _____ Purpose _____ Location/Institution _____ When Projected to Start and End ___ _____ 2. Competency Area _____ Purpose _____ Location/Institution _____ When Projected to Start and End ___ _____	1. Employer _____ Position _____ Reason _____ 2. Employer _____ Position _____ Reason _____
Long-term (Education and Training)	**Long-term (Career)**
3. Competency Area _____ Purpose _____ Location/Institution _____ When Projected to Start and End ___ _____ 4. Competency Area _____ Purpose _____ Location/Institution _____ When Projected to Start and End ___ _____	3. Employer _____ Position _____ Reason _____ 4. Employer _____ Position _____ Reason _____

COMMUNITY ACTIVITIES/ORGANIZATIONS AND CLUBS

Activity	Responsibility	Office Held (if any)

HONORS AND AWARDS

Outside Back Cover

WORKPLACE BASICS

(Listed below are the skills and abilities employers want their employees to have. Identify the skill you have acquired in each area, or identify the skill you need.)

	Skill I Have	Skill I Need
Reading Skills. Skills involving use of printed resource material for obtaining and applying information.		
Writing Skills. Skills involving written communication of processes, information, or ideas.		
Mathematics Skills. Skills involving computation, calculation, or interpretation of numerical data.		
Science Skills. Skills involving mastery and application of scientific information or theory.		
Oral Communication Skills. Skills involving speaking and listening.		
Interpersonal or Relating Skills. Skills involving working and getting along with others, working in teams, leadership, and negotiation.		
Creative Thinking and Problem-Solving Skills. Skills involving comprehending, applying, analyzing, and developing complex ideas and situations.		
Employability Skills. Skills involving choosing, obtaining, and succeeding in a career.		
Social Studies Skills. Skills involving investigation and application of social concepts.		

Interviewing

For many of us, interviews are the most fearsome part of finding a job, but they are also our best chance to show an employer our qualifications. Interviews are far more flexible than application forms or tests. Use that flexibility to your advantage. You can reduce your anxiety and improve your performance by preparing for your interviews ahead of time.

Begin by considering what interviewers want to know. You represent a risk to the employer. A hiring mistake is expensive in terms of lost productivity, wasted training costs, and the cost of finding a replacement. To lessen the risk, interviewers try to select people who are highly motivated, understand what the job entails, and show that their background has prepared them for the work involved.

You show that you are highly motivated by learning about the company before the interview, by dressing appropriately, and by being well-mannered: You greet the interviewer by name, you do not chew gum or smoke, you listen attentively, and you thank the interviewer at the end of the session. You also show motivation by expressing interest in the job at the end of the interview.

You show that you understand what the job entails and that you can handle it when you explain how your qualifications have prepared you for specific duties described in the company's job listing, and when you ask intelligent questions about the nature of the work and the training provided for new workers.

One of the best ways to prepare for an interview is to have some practice sessions with a friend. Here is a list of some of the most commonly asked questions to get you started.

- ★ Why did you apply for this job?
- ★ What do you know about this job or company?
- ★ Why did you choose this career?

★ Why should I hire you?

★ What would you do if (usually filled in with a work-related crisis)?

★ How would you describe yourself?

★ What would you like to tell me about yourself?

★ What are your major strengths?

★ What are your major weaknesses?

★ What type of work do you like least?

★ What accomplishment gave you the greatest satisfaction?

★ What was your worst mistake?

★ What would you change in your life?

★ What courses and training did you like best or least?

★ What did you like best or least about your military service?

★ Why did you leave the military?

★ How does your education or experience relate to this job?

★ What are your goals?

★ How do you plan to reach them?

★ What do you hope to be doing in five years? In ten years?

★ What salary do you expect?

Essentially, your strategy should be to concentrate on the job and your ability to do it no matter what the question seems to be asking. If asked for a strength, mention something job-related. If asked for a weakness, mention a job-related strength (you work too hard, you worry too much about details, you always have to see the big picture). If asked about a disability or a specific negative factor in your past—a criminal record, being fired—be prepared to stress what you learned from the experience, how you have overcome the shortcoming, and how you are now in a position to do a better job.

So far, only the interviewer's questions have been discussed. But an interview will be a two-way conversation. You really do need to learn more about the position to find out if you want the job. Given how frustrating it is to look for a job, you do not want to take just any position only to learn two weeks later that you can't stand the place and have to look for another job right away. Here are some questions for you to ask the interviewer.

★ What would a day on this job be like?

★ To whom would I report? May I meet this person?

★ Would I supervise anyone? May I meet them?

★ How important is this job to the company?

★ What training programs are offered?

★ What advancement opportunities are offered?

★ Why did the last person leave this job?

★ What is that person doing now?

★ What is the greatest challenge of this position?

★ What plans does the company have with regard to (mention some development of which you have read or heard)?

★ Is the company growing?

After you ask such questions, listen to the interviewer's answers and then, if at all possible, point to something in your education or experience related to it. You might notice that questions about salary and fringe benefits are not included in this list. Your focus at a first interview should be on the company and what you will do for it, not what it will pay you. The salary range will often be given in the ad or position announcement, and information on the usual fringe benefits will be available from the personnel department. Once you have been offered a position, you can negotiate the salary. Job hunting guides available in bookstores and at the library give many more hints on this subject.

As you are preparing your strategies and career credentials for becoming a free agent in today's open labor market, also examine what employers are looking for today in midmanagement or supervisory-level employees. These characteristics need to serve as a blueprint to preparing your portfolio to assure that job negotiations will be in your favor.

The following are worker characteristics that employers are most impressed with:

★ Training that is recent, credible, and reflects today's workplace.

★ Work record that shows responsibility, dependability, productivity, creativity, and stability.

★ Commitment to past employers as evidenced by long-term employment and upward growth in career field.

★ Stability of nonwork life with little evidence of social, political, or family problems.

★ Willingness to learn and take risks to be creative.

★ Self-starter with a mature ability to make judgments and decisions.

★ Desire to experiment and venture into job opportunities that might have risks. Setbacks are useful learning experiences.

★ Current knowledge of your career field; how your knowledge applies to their company.

You have most or many of these "in-demand" characteristics. Your task, as your own marketing agent, is to communicate these strengths in such a way that the employer will see them and understand the advantages in their company. It is difficult for most of us to spend time looking at ourselves and our past achievements to create a self-serving, positive picture, but that's what employment marketing is all about. You know best how good you are; the trick is to convey this in a way the employer will believe.

Impressing an Employer
★★

Consider being a personnel manager drowning under a flood of job applicants competing for the same opportunity. With your busy schedule, what would make you select one highly qualified applicant over another? Employers suggest that the following information and interview performance can make the difference.

★ Have a record of your training experience.

★ Verbalize a good knowledge of the company.

★ Have a record of your work performance.

★ Know what you want; you won't take just anything.

★ Put this job into the context of your career goals.

★ Have letters of recommendation.

★ Be prepared to say "yes" to training requirements.

★ Know what you need for a salary and know your bottom line.

★ Have all credentials (papers) in a neat, well-organized portfolio.

★ Be prepared to leave a copy with the employer.

★ Exhibit a presence of knowing exactly what you want and indicate how this job could fulfill your needs perfectly.

Look at the top three items in the chart on page 224—the items that employers responded to most positively. These items reflect how a person looks and behaves at the time of the application and interview. They are job-search skills that anyone can have and that give employers their first impression of you.

First impressions count. Everything you do—or don't do—sends signals to employers. You want to send signals that give them the following messages:

★ I am very interested in this job.

★ I take pride in myself and what I do.

★ I have respect for employers.

★ I have a sense of purpose and direction.

Such messages are sent in a variety of ways.

Your Appearance

Make a point of being clean, neat, well-groomed, and appropriately dressed. Dress conservatively. Don't wear trendy or dramatic clothes to the interview. Give employers the impression that you are a serious, responsible, and respectful person. Your clothes can say a lot about your attitude and behavior.

The Job Application

Complete the job application neatly and accurately. Make sure you know (or have with you) any information the employer might request, such as your Social Security number or references. Have an erasable ink pen with you, so if you make a mistake, you will be able to correct it neatly. Leave no blank spaces on the application. If something doesn't apply to you, write "N/A" (not applicable) in the blank. Take your time. Proofread the application when you are finished.

Your Resumé

Prepare a resumé that you can attach to every job application. A resumé is another way to advertise your good qualities—your achievements, special skills, and good character.

The Interview

Try to express a good attitude during the interview. One way is to ask questions about the job and the company. This shows your interest and motivation. Be positive in all you say. For example, ask, "What are the hours that you expect me to work?" or "Are there opportunities to work extra hours?" Avoid questions that may signal a negative attitude, such as, "Do I have to work on Saturdays?" Your facial expression, tone of voice, and posture should reflect a positive attitude also.

The Follow-Up

Telephone the employer after the interview to show your interest. Make your call brief, to the point, and pleasant. Thank the employer for having the chance to interview with him or her. Say that you are very interested in the job. This keeps you in the employer's mind and confirms your interest in the job.

Things That Are Important to Interviewers

Scale

Very Important

★ Looked clean and neat at the interview

★ Filled out the job application neatly and correctly

★ Attached a complete resumé to the job application

★ Phoned the employer after the interview to show interest in getting the job

★ Asked many questions about the job or company during the interview

★ Had a previous employer who would rehire him or her

★ Had training in the job skills needed for this job but no experience

★ Had a background in math and science

Least Important

★ Understood that he or she might need to start at a low level

Your Abilities

Employers also want evidence of your ability to do the job. You can give them that evidence by mentioning these points:

★ **References.** If your previous supervisor thought well of you and your work, say so. Suggest that the employer call that supervisor to learn about your performance on the job. Make sure you ask the supervisor's permission to use his or her name before you provide it. Also, know the addresses and phone numbers of any reference you will use. You will need to give this information to the employer.

★ **Training.** If you have had special training in the military that is specific to the job, tell the employer about it. Explain where you got the training and exactly what it involved. Mention the kinds of equipment you used. Job training works in your favor, especially if you have no civilian work experience. It may signal to an employer that you know the demands and conditions of the industry and have a real interest in working there.

★ **Education.** Explain how the courses you have taken relate to the job you are seeking. Employers want to see the relationship of your education to the jobs they are trying to fill.

★ **Work experience.** Indicate all types of work experience—paid and non-paid. The important thing you are trying to convey is that you can do the job. Every job requires planning, effort, and skill. Explain the work you have done. Describe the tasks involved and the skills you have developed through your military service.

What Not to Do
★★

The chart on page 226 shows the order in which employers ranked the negative effects of information and behavior observed during interviews. Their average rankings ranged from "very negative" to "somewhat negative."

Things That Have a Negative Effect on Interviewers

Scale

Very Negative

★ Gave false information on the job application

★ Could not read a newspaper

★ Had been absent from previous job 12 different times

★ Had been 15 percent less productive than other workers in the last position because he or she was not trying

★ Had three jobs in the last six months

★ Was late for the interview appointment

★ Got confused when asked a simple question

★ Used poor grammar when speaking

★ Had been 15 percent less productive than other workers in the last position even though he or she was trying

Somewhat Negative

★ Had never worked in the civilian labor market before

The employers saw all of the items on the chart as negatives for the applicant. But the behaviors at the top of the list were viewed as the most serious problems and would probably influence the employer against hiring a specific person. Certainly, few employers would hire someone who lied on the application. You can avoid the temptation to lie by doing the following:

★ **Think before you answer a question.** What are employers seeking when they ask, "Why do you want the job?" Many of them are asking, "Are you serious about working?" "Will you like the work?" "Will you work hard?" "Will you stay with the job or will you quit soon?" Employers don't want to know very personal facts about you or your family. Just answer the question briefly and honestly.

★ **Know you have value.** Put yourself in the best light. For example, you might be applying for a job at a specified sporting goods store because it is near your home and you won't have to fight the downtown traffic. Also, you might like selling merchandise and working with people. If so, tell the employer all these facts, not just one of them. Don't say, "I hate driving in traffic, so I am applying here." That is not very positive, nor is it totally true. Instead, say, "I chose your store because it is convenient to my home, and I know I would enjoy selling the merchandise and working with people." Don't be tempted to lie to impress the employer. Don't say, "I know all about camping gear" if you don't. The employer will soon find out! Employers don't expect you to know everything, so don't feel you have to be more than you are.

★ **Be positive when describing yourself and your efforts.** If you do have to explain a problem in your background, do it in a positive way. For example, suppose the employer asks you to explain why you are still looking for work six months after your release date. Don't tell the employer that you have been waiting for the right job to come along. This might lead an employer to think that you sat at home watching television and waiting for a job. Instead, tell the employer you have been applying for jobs. Mention specific things you have done during your period of unemployment, such as taking a relevant course. Your answer should show that you are industrious, conscientious, and serious about your future.

Using Your Advantages
★★

The following is a list of what employers consider "most important" attributes of excellent workers. Your military experience has probably left you with most of these. Look them over and be prepared to impress the employer that you have all or most of these 35 characteristics.

1. You consider the needs of the public and others over your personal needs.

2. You are considerate. You try to understand other people's positions.

3. You are friendly and sociable.

4. You are cooperative.

5. You can take the lead. You are capable of serving as a leader.

6. You are courteous.

7. You follow directions carefully.

8. You are guided by good common sense and follow rules and regulations.

9. You are cheerful.

10. You are witty and humorous.

11. You are courageous

12. You are patient.

13. You have a strong sense of responsibility.

14. You have a strong will and usually finish a job you start.

15. You are good at making profits.

16. You are honest.

17. You like work that is full of variety.

18. You are enthusiastic abut doing things.

19. You are quick at doing things.

20. You are careful when doing things.

21. You are quick to understand ideas and can make good judgments.

22. You have a sense of justice and fair play.

23. You can take prompt actions in emergency situations.

24. You do things accurately and in an orderly manner.

25. You think about your future and make good plans for it.

26. You are creative.

27. You are adventurous.

28. You can express yourself well orally.

29. You can express yourself well in writing.

30. You can write legibly.

31. You maintain good personal grooming habits.

32. You have a good memory.

33. You are capable of teaching things to others.

34. You can copy words and figures and detect errors.

35. You can calculate quickly.

Your military experience and record give you your first big advantage over other individuals in the civilian labor market. Also, the fact that the armed forces train and retrain in job areas that match well with the civilian market gives you a second advantage. Your age makes you extremely valuable because the risk of job hopping and poor performance due to lack of experience gives you an additional edge. Employers also value the high expectations and standardization that is present in the military. The fact that you work well under these conditions relates to great savings for them.

The following is a suggested approach to ensure that you become the applicant of choice early in the job interview:

★ Study the style, requirements, and operation of the business you'd like to work for. (The library has reference material on the businesses in your area.)

★ Examine your style, skills, interests, needs, and requirements for your new career (from your work in Chapters 5 and 6).

★ Compare these two points and see where they come together. If they don't, then why apply? If they do, then your approach to an interview is to prepare good answers and credentials on each issue.

★ Go to the job interview fully prepared. The interviewer needs to see immediately that you cared enough about your career and his or her time to prepare well. Surprise the interviewer with special knowledge about the company (not normally expected), and show self-confidence.

★ When issues of training ability, past performance, recommendations, training received, or career goals come up in the interview, you need to have documentation ready to present and leave behind.

Your confidence, sense of direction, and knowledge of yourself and the company will make most interviewers remember you before your competitors.

At the end of the interview, you should know what the next step will be: Whether you should contact the interviewer again, whether you should provide more information, whether more interviews must be conducted, and when a final decision will be reached. Try to end on a positive note by reaffirming your interest in the position and pointing out why you will be a good choice to fill it.

Immediately after the interview, make notes of what went well and what you would like to improve. To show your interest in the position, send a follow-up letter to the interviewer, providing further information on some point raised in the interview and thanking the interviewer once again. Remember, someone is going to hire you; it might be the person you just talked to.

Selecting the Best Offer
★★★

One interesting and positive frustration you'll experience, if you're applying to several businesses, is that you may receive more than one offer. You'll need to give a timely response, so you need to be ready to make quick, sound judgments and decisions. The following are key issues that should be applied to your decision making.

★ Salary	★ Training opportunities
★ Fringe benefits	★ Travel opportunities
★ Career ladder potential	★ Services for family
★ Location	★ Vacation time
★ Healthy environment	★ Management/supervisor
★ Stability of firm	

Use the goals and priorities you set in Chapters 5 and 6 in considering the following principles:

★ Decide what your conditions are and prioritize them.

★ Using some form of checklist, listing your factors, take detailed notes during the interview.

★ Immediately after the interview, rate the job potential in preparation for your "yes" or "no" response to the employer.

Self-Assessment
★★

Before you go to your next interview, use the checklist and worksheet on the following pages to help yourself prepare.

Summary Checklist

Did you:

☐ Find out the name of the interviewer?

☐ Find out the location of the interview?

☐ Find out the date and time of the interview?

☐ Find out where to park?

☐ Make arrangements for children?

☐ Make arrangements for transportation?

☐ Determine the amount of time you need to get to the interview?

☐ Identify the time you must leave for the interview?

☐ Anticipate questions you may be asked and prepare answers to those questions?

   ☐ Present a positive appearance?

   ☐ Shower and shave?

   ☐ Use deodorant?

   ☐ Wash, comb, and style your hair?

   ☐ Use limited amount of makeup?

   ☐ Use perfume or aftershave lotion sparingly?

   ☐ Brush your teeth?

   ☐ Appear rested?

   ☐ Appear calm?

   ☐ Appear to be in good health?

   ☐ Wear clothing that was clean and well pressed?

Did you:

☐ Choose clothes of the correct style and length?

☐ Wear conservative clothing?

☐ Take a copy of your resumé?

☐ Take a copy of your prepared message?

☐ Take samples of your work?

☐ Leave for the interview alone and at the scheduled departure time?

☐ Arrive at least ten minutes early?

☐ Call the interviewer if you were delayed or ill?

☐ Greet the interviewer?

   ☐ Stand erect and appear confident?

   ☐ Look at the interviewer and smile?

   ☐ Shake hands with a firm grip?

   ☐ Use the interviewer's full name?

☐ Complete the introductions?

   ☐ Introduce yourself, using your full name?

   ☐ Explain why you were in his or her office?

   ☐ Speak clearly?

   ☐ Show enthusiasm in your voice and manner?

   ☐ Act self-assured and confident?

   ☐ Act pleasant and respectful?

   ☐ Wait for the interviewer to ask you to be seated?

continued

Did you:

- ☐ Ask if you may be seated if the interviewer did not suggest it?
- ☐ Maintain good posture?
- ☐ Explain why you wanted the job and why you were suited for it?
- ☐ Think before answering questions?
- ☐ Avoid saying things you didn't mean to say?
- ☐ Answer questions directly and honestly without providing unnecessary details?
- ☐ Answer questions in a positive way?
- ☐ Avoid mentioning negative facts?
- ☐ Ask questions if you did not understand what was said?
- ☐ Use proper terminology?
- ☐ Use correct grammar?
- ☐ Use proper vocabulary? (Avoid using slang words and offensive words?)
- ☐ Speak courteously in a pleasant tone of voice?
- ☐ Speak clearly, pronouncing words carefully?
- ☐ Vary expression in your voice?
- ☐ Maintain good posture during the interview?
- ☐ Give your full attention to the interviewer?
- ☐ Use your facial expression to show interest and enthusiasm?
- ☐ Avoid smoking or chewing gum?

Did you:

- ☐ Find out the department or area of the company where you might work?
- ☐ Find out the specific job tasks you would be asked to do?
- ☐ Find out the hours you would work?
- ☐ Find out about promotional opportunities?
- ☐ Find out about the company's volume of business?
- ☐ Find out about the types of customers the business serves?
- ☐ Find out about the scope of the company's activities?
- ☐ Sense when the interviewer wished to close the interview? (Watch for the interviewer to stand or to say he or she would be in contact with you?)
- ☐ Express your interest in the company?
- ☐ Explain that you would be interviewing in other places?
- ☐ Tell the interviewer that you would call back within the week?
- ☐ Ask what day or time would be best to call?
- ☐ Record any facts on a sheet of paper?
- ☐ Leave a copy of your resumé?
- ☐ Invite the interviewer to call you at the listed number?
- ☐ Smile and thank the interviewer for his or her time and effort?
- ☐ Shake hands and leave?

Interview Question Worksheet

The following are typical questions that interviewers ask. Develop answers in advance, jot them down on the form so you can review them before your interview.

Tell me about yourself. _____
_____

Why should you be our choice? _____
_____

Are you a good worker? Why? _____
_____

What kind of work are you looking for? _____
_____

What are your career goals? _____
_____
_____

What do you do in your leisure time? _____
_____

What are two or three of your strengths and weaknesses? ___
_____

What are two or three limitations you may have? _____
_____

What was the greatest benefit you gained from your military experience?
_____

What benefits can you bring to this company? _____
_____

What do you expect us to do for you? _____
_____

What do you know about this company? _____
_____

Why do you want to work for this company? _____
_____

continued

How would you handle conflict with supervisors or fellow workers? ____

____

What part of your military service did you like best? ____

____

What questions were you hoping I'd ask? ____

____

Source: Army National Guard, *Go For It*.

Follow-Up Communication

In Chapters 12 and 13, a number of ideas were offered on how to penetrate the labor market. One mistake we often make is following up on all initial leads, whether in writing, by phone, or in person. The issue here is that personnel managers get hundreds of letters, calls, applications, and walk-ins from people who are interested in either a specific job or the company in general. You are often just a blur on the manager's computer screen, and you must direct his or her attention to your name and credentials. This is true if you have already taken a job, if you were turned down, or if you have not heard anything.

The follow-up is always important because you never know when you might be looking for work again, and you want to leave a good impression. You want your name to be recognized. You want to remembered as the person who went the extra distance.

What does a follow-up contact suggest to the personnel manager? It means that you have the following qualities:

★ Confidence

★ Perseverence

★ Professional behavior

★ Respect (for personnel officer)

★ Organization

★ Good communication

Let's look at the different types of follow-up techniques.

Written Correspondence
★★★

There are four types of correspondence that you may find yourself using:

1. A note letting the employer know that you have received the information concerning your interview, and will be in their office on a specific date and time.

2. A postinterview letter before you receive word of their decision. Thanking the interviewers for their interest and time, and then highlighting a unique characteristic that you feel might be important for the job, is very effective. You may also include information that you did not provide during the interview, but that you feel is important.

3. A letter after you have received a rejection, thanking them for consideration and stating that you are interested in future opportunities.

4. A letter letting the interviewer know that you have accepted a position elsewhere.

Telephone or Fax
★★★

Often you will get through to the person you want to talk to, but having your name on a phone slip or a fax message helps the personnel staff remember your name. The phone or fax could be used for almost all of the situations given in the preceding correspondence section. The phone or fax speeds up the process; timing may be of the essence in a job hunt.

Remember that some personnel staff may be annoyed with phone calls, especially if you are persistent. You do not want to put the person in an uncomfortable position while they are still making a decision.

Drop In
★★★

You need to be very selective about dropping in to see someone with whom you have interviewed or a person who did not call but with whom you wanted an interview. The reasons for a visit with the personnel office staff could be the following:

1. You want to learn how to better yourself in future interviews.

2. You want to register the fact that, although you did not get a particular position, you are interested in future openings.

3. You want to thank the person for being so professional and helpful at the interview.

Rules

★★

Follow-ups need to be short, very specific, timely, and to the point; they should not look like arm twisters. A potted plant, free tickets to a baseball game, or a free car-wash coupon are not acceptable. There are three rules in this aspect of job hunting:

1. Be professional

2. Be professional

3. Be professional

The following are some targeted paragraphs that could be used in mail, fax, or phone follow-up communications.

In reviewing the interview I had with you for the position of graphic designer, I wanted you to know how helpful and professional you were. Talking with you made me even more interested in the position, because now I can see career growth opportunities that were not evident before.

I am following up on my letter of interest and credential package I sent to you on July 2 for the position of computer programmer. As I am sure you can appreciate, I applied for more than one job in the city. Although I haven't heard from your office and I remain interested in your company, please be advised that I have taken the position of Chief Programmer at the INET Corporation. I would appreciate you keeping my records for future reference.

Thank you for your phone call of July 2 indicating that I was not selected for the position of fashion designer. Although I am disappointed, I request that you keep my credentials on file for future job openings. After the interview, I realized I brought the wrong portfolio examples for the job you had available. I learned from this experience, and I want you to know that I do have past experience and outstanding examples of my work to show you on the next occasion.

Although these examples are only lead paragraphs for longer letters, they give you examples of pointed and professional communication.

The following points are key to good follow-up communications:

1. All communication should be brief, to the point, and timely.

2. Communication should be personal but professional.

3. Do not rehash the interview.

4. Do not suggest frustration or anger.

5. Do not be pushy, overbearing, or egotistical.

Remember, if the follow-up communication doesn't give you added value, don't communicate.

APPENDIXES

★★★★★★★★★★★★★★★★★★

The following organizations and references can provide you with all the information you need to get started in civilian life. Good research is the basis of any successful job search, so make use of these valuable resources.

Appendix 1

Military Organizations

National Service Organizations
★★★

American Legion .... Indianapolis, IN 46206

American National Red Cross .... Washington, DC 20006

AMVETS .... Washington, DC 20036

Blinded Veterans' Association .... Washington, DC 20037

Congressional Medal of Honor Society of
the U.S.A. .... Braintree, MA 02184

Disabled American Veterans .... Cincinnati, OH 45214

Legion of Valor of the United States of
America, Inc. .... Arlington, VA 22204

Marine Corps League .... Arlington, VA 22201

Military Order of the Purple Heart .... Washington, DC 20013

Paralyzed Veterans of America, Inc. .... Washington, DC 20420

United Spanish War Veterans .... Washington, DC 20420

Veterans of Foreign Wars of the United
States .... Kansas City, MO 64111

Veterans of World War I of the U.S.A.,
Inc. .... Alexandria, VA 22314

Other National Service Organizations Recognized by the VA
★★

Air Force Sergeants' Association .... Marlow Heights, MD 22031

American Veterans' Committee .... Washington, DC 20036

Army and Navy Union, U.S.A. .... Lakemore, OH 44250

Army Mutual Aid Association .... Arlington, VA 22211

Catholic War Veterans of the U.S.A. .... Washington, DC 20001

Coast Guard League .... Washington, DC 20591

Disabled Officers' Association .... Washington, DC 20006

Fleet Reserve Association .... Washington, DC 20036

Jewish War Veterans of the United States .. Washington, DC 20009

Military Order of the World Wars .... Washington, DC 20006

National Jewish Welfare Board .... New York, NY 10010

National Tribune .... Washington, DC 20013

Navy Mutual Aid Association .... Washington, DC 20370

Regular Veterans' Association .... Washington, DC 20015

United Indian War Veterans, U.S.A. .... San Francisco, CA 94103

Other Military Service–Related Organizations
★★

Air Force Association (AFA) .... Arlington, VA 22209

Armed Forces Communications and
Electronics Association .... Fairfax, VA 22033

Association of the United States Army
(AUSA) .... Arlington, VA 22210

Marine Corps Association (MCA) .... Quantico, VA 22134

Marine Corps Reserve Officers' Association
(MCROA) .... Alexandria, VA 22314

Marine Executive Association (MEA) .... McLean, VA 22102

Navy League of the United States .... Arlington, VA 22201

Non-commissioned Officers' Association
(NCOA) .... Alexandria, VA 22314

The Retired Officers' Association .... Alexandria, VA 22314

West Point Alumni Association .... West Point, NY 10996

State Organizations Recognized by the VA

★★

Alabama Department of Veterans' Affairs .. Montgomery, AL 36102

Alaska Division of Veterans' Affairs .... Juneau, AK 99811

Arizona—Department of Economic
Security .... Phoenix, AZ 85007

Arkansas—Veterans' Service Office .... Little Rock, AR 72201

California—Department of Veterans'
Affairs .... Sacramento, CA 95828

Colorado—Department of Social Services .. Denver, CO 80202

Connecticut—Soldiers, Sailors, and Marine
Fund .... Hartford, CT 06115

District of Columbia—Office of Veterans'
Affairs .... Washington, DC 20004

Florida—Division of Veterans' Affairs .... St. Petersburg, FL 33731

Georgia—Department of Veterans' Service .. Atlanta, GA 30334

Hawaii—Department of Social Services ..... Honolulu, HI 96809

Idaho—Division of Veterans' Services .... Boise, ID 83707

Illinois—Department of Veterans' Affairs .. Springfield, IL 62705

Kansas—Veterans' Commission .... Topeka, KS 66612

Kentucky—Center for Veterans' Affairs .... Louisville, KY 40203

Louisiana—Department of Veterans'
Affairs .... Baton Rouge, LA 70801

Maine—Bureau of Veterans' Services .... Augusta, ME 04330

Maryland—Veterans' Service Commission .. Baltimore, MD 21201

Massachusetts—Office of Commissioner of
Veterans' Service .... Boston, MA 02002

Minnesota—Department of Veterans'
Affairs .... St. Paul, MN 55101

Mississippi—Veterans' Affairs Commission .. Jackson, MS 39205

Missouri—Division of Veterans' Affairs ..... Jefferson City, MO 65101

Montana—Veterans' Affairs Division .... Helena, MT 59601

Nebraska—Department of Veterans' Affairs . Lincoln, NE 65809

Nevada—Commission of Veterans' Affairs .. Reno, NV 89502

New Hampshire—State Veterans' Council .. Concord, NH 03306

New Jersey—Division of Veterans' Service .. Trenton, NJ 08625

New Mexico—Veterans' Service
Commission .... Santa Fe, NM 87501

New York—Division of Veterans' Affairs .. New York, NY 10010

North Carolina—Division of Veterans'
Affairs .... Raleigh, NC 26701

North Dakota—Department of Veterans'
Affairs .... Fargo, ND 58102

Ohio—Division of Soldiers' Claims and
Veterans' Affairs .... Columbus, OH 43215

Oklahoma—Department of Veterans'
Affairs .... Oklahoma City, OK 73105

Oregon—Department of Veterans' Affairs .. Salem, OR 97301

Pennsylvania—Department of Military
Affairs .... Harrisburg, PA 17108

Puerto Rico—Department of Labor,
Veterans' Office .... Hato Rey, PR 00917

Rhode Island—Veterans Affairs .... Providence, RI 02903

South Carolina—Department of Veterans'
Affairs .... Columbia, SC 29201

South Dakota—Division of Veterans'
Affairs .... Pierre, SD 57501

Tennessee—Department of Veterans'
Affairs .... Nashville, TN 37203

Texas—Veterans' Affairs Commission .... Austin, TX 78711

Utah—Office of Veterans' Services .... Salk Lake City, UT 84111

Vermont—Veterans' Affairs Section,
Military Department .... Montpelier, VT 05602

Virginia—Division of War Veterans' Claims . Roanoke, VA 24011

Washington—Department of Veterans'
Affairs .... Olympia, WA 98501

West Virginia—Department of Veterans'
Affairs .... Charleston, WV 25305

Wisconsin—Department of Veterans'
Affairs .... Madison, WI 53702

Territories
★★

American Samoa—Veterans' Affairs Office .. Pago Pago, American
Samoa

Guam—Office of Veterans' Affairs .... Agana, Guam 96910

Virgin Islands—Department of Veterans'   Christiansted, St. Croix,
Affairs .... Virgin Islands 08820

Appendix 2

Recommended Reading

If you have time and want to do some additional reading to develop your employment transition skills, consider the following resources:

Bastress, Francis. *Guide to Employment: Options and Strategies in the U.S. and Abroad.* Woodley Publications, 1994.

Beatty, Richard H. *Interviewing and Selecting High Performers.* New York: John Wiley and Sons, Inc., 1994.

Garlock, Michael. *From Soldier to Civilian, How to Use Military Job Training to Get a Civilian Job.* New York: Prentice-Hall Trade (ARCO), 1988.

Kennedy, Joyce Lain, and Thomas J. Morrow. *Electronic Job Search Revolution.* New York: John Wiley and Sons, Inc., 1994.

Kennedy, Joyce Lain, and Thomas J. Morrow. *Electronic Resumé Revolution: Creating a Winning Resumé for the New World of Job Seeking.* New York: John Wiley and Sons, Inc., 1994.

"Civilian Again, #7016, *Life Skills Education.* (A series of guidebooks on a range of career transitional issues), Northfield, MN: 1994.

Nadler, Burton Jay. *Noted at the Interview: Tips and Quizzes to Prepare You for Your First Job Interview.* New York: John Wiley and Sons, Inc., 1994.

Nyman, Keith O. *Re-entry: How to Build on Your Military Experience with Civilian Success.* Harrisburg, PA: Stackpole Books, 1981.

Occupational Briefs—600 Occupations to Choose From. Moravia, NY: Chronicle Guidance Publications, Inc.

Occupational Outlook Handbook. Lincolnwood, IL: VGM Career Horizons, 1994.

Successful Job Search Strategies for the Disabled. New York: John Wiley and Sons, Inc., 1994.

Appendix 3

Resources and Assistance

Detailed information about actual addresses and phone numbers at the state level are beyond the scope of this book, but the following national office listings may be useful.

★ **Information about jobs/training.**

> National Occupational Information Coordinating Committee
> 2100 M Street, NW
> Washington, DC 20037
> 202/653-5665

★ **Veterans' affairs/benefits.** Don't write. Call for state and regional offices. 202/872-1151 (national office)

★ **Veterans' affairs centers.** The government listings in your phone book will give you up-to-date addresses and phone numbers.

★ **Alternative teacher certification programs.** Available in 23 states and growing to help offset teacher shortages. Call your Veterans' Affairs Office for specific information in your location.

★ **Federal job information centers.** Most states have offices that are connected to the Office of Personnel Management (OPM). Check your phone book or write to

> U.S. OPM
> Federal Job Information Center
> 1900 E Street, NW
> Washington, DC 20415

★ **Small business development.** Every state and many cities have branches of the Small Business Administration. Your phone book is your best source of information, but you can also call 800/365-5855.

★ **Apprenticeship training.** Each state department of labor or its job service office can provide detailed information. See the government listings in your local phone book or write

> Federal Office of Apprenticeship and Training
> 200 Constitution Avenue, NW
> Washington, DC 20210
> 202/535-0545

★ **Veterans' Employment and Training Service.** Your state department of labor or local job service office is your best source of information.

★ **Job Training Partnership Act.** This is a $3 billion fund for retraining. Start by writing

> The National Association of Private Industry
> 1201 New York Avenue, NW, Room 800
> Washington, DC 20005
> 202/289-2950

★ **U.S. Peace Corps.** For those who want to volunteer, write

> U.S. Peace Corps.
> 1990 K Street, NW
> Washington, DC 20526
> 800/424-8580

Other information sources include the following:

★ Your public library, which has directories and computer programs about schools and related financial aid

★ The counselor at your local high school or community college

★ Your local job service office (U.S. Employment Service)

★ The American Association of Junior and Community Colleges (202/293-7050)

★ The Association of Independent Colleges and Schools (202/659-2460)

★ The National Association of Trade and Technical Schools (202/333-1021)

Appendix 4

Veterans' Benefits

The following list is not all-inclusive, but the point is that you have resources for counseling, training, or small business development if you need them. The best source of benefit information is your local or state office of Veterans' Employment and Training Service connected with the Department of Labor. The timetable on pages 252 through 256 provides some more descriptive information about your possible benefits, the time factors involved, and whom you should contact.

★ **GI Bill.** some restrictions apply, based on service time.

★ **Montgomery GI Bill.**

★ **Education institutions.** A variety of specialized loans, scholarships, and grants, some of which favor the veteran, are available.

★ **Farm Cooperative Program.** Twelve months of training costs are covered.

★ **Apprenticeship training.** Fifty-five percent of course costs is covered.

★ **Correspondence training.** Fifty-five percent of course costs is covered.

★ **GED.** Veterans are eligible for basic entitlement.

★ **Tutorial assistance.** $100 per month, up to $1,200 is available.

★ **Educational loans.** Up to $2,500 per academic year with low interest can be borrowed, based upon need.

★ **VEAP.** Some of you have contributed to this special training fund.

★ **Vocational rehabilitation.** Benefits are excellent if you are eligible, but there are restrictions.

★ **Pension Recipients Vocational Training Benefit.** Up to 24 months of training cost covered.

★ **VA–Home Buying Loan Guarantees.**

★ **Home loans for the disabled.**

★ **Veterans readjustment counseling services.**

★ **Unemployment compensation for ex-service personnel.**

Veterans Benefits Timetable

Time Frame	Benefits	Where to Apply
10 years from release from active duty	**Montgomery GI Bill:** Eligible participants first entering active duty 7/1/85 through 6/30/88, or with old GI Bill eligibility meeting minimum service requirements, may receive financial assistance to go to college or a vocational program. Vocational and educational counseling is available on request.	Any VA office
10 years from release from active duty	**VEAP (Post-Vietnam Era Veterans' Education Assistance Program):** If you entered service on or after 1/1/77 and participated in the voluntary contributory program while on active duty, the VA may pay you benefits while you pursue an approved program of education and training. Vocational and educational counseling is available on request. Maximum length of payment is 36 months or the number of months contributions were made, whichever is less.	Any VA office
12 years (generally from date of notice of VA disability rating)	**Vocational Rehabilitation:** If you have a disability that was incurred in or aggravated by military service, you may be eligible for vocational rehabilitation services to assist you in overcoming your employment handicap and become better able to handle day-to-day living activities. As part of a rehabilitation program, the VA will pay your tuition, fees, books, tools, and other expenses, as	Any VA office

continued

Time Frame	Benefits	*Where to Apply*
	well as provide you with a monthly living allowance. Once you have taken part in a vocational rehabilitation program, the VA will help you get a job. A seriously disabled veteran may be provided with services and assistance to increase independence in daily living.	
No time limit	**GI loans:** The VA will guarantee your loan for the purchase of a house or condominium, or the building of a new house.	Any VA office
No time limit	**Disability compensation:** The VA pays compensation for disabilities incurred in or aggravated by military service. Payments are made from the date of separation if a claim is filed within one year.	Any VA office
No time limit	**Medical care:** The VA provides a full range of medical care benefits, including help for alcoholism and other drug dependency to service-connected veterans and to nonservice connected veterans who meet certain eligibility criteria. Readjustment counseling benefits are also available at VA Veterans' Centers for eligible Vietnam-era veterans. Outpatient treatment is available for all service-connected conditions.	Any VA office or medical center
90 days	**Dental treatment:** The VA provides necessary dental care for veterans who were not given a dental examination and treatment within 90 days of discharge or separation from service. The time limit does not apply to veterans with dental disabilities resulting from combat wounds or service injuries.	Any VA office or medical center

continued

Time Frame	*Benefits*	*Where to Apply*
Within 90 days of separation	**One-time dental treatment.** The VA provides one-time treatment dental care for certain service-connected dental conditions.	Any VA office or VA hospital
1 year from date of notice of VA disability rating	**GI insurance:** Low-cost life insurance (up to $10,000) is available for veterans with service-connected disabilities. Veterans who are totally disabled may apply for a waiver of premiums on these policies.	Any VA office
120 days, or up to 12 years if totally disabled	**SGLI (Servicemen's Group Life Insurance):** This may be converted to VGLI (Veteran's Group Life Insurance), a five-year nonrenewable term policy. At the end of the five-year term, VGLI may be converted to an individual policy with any participating insurance company. The VA can provide more information.	Office of Servicemen's Group Life Insurance 213 Washington Street Newark, NJ 07102
No time limit	**Employment:** Assistance is available in finding employment in private industry, federal service, and local government.	Local or state employment service, U.S. Office of Personnel management or any VA office
Limited time	**Unemployment compensation:** The amount of benefits and payment periods vary among states. Apply soon after separation.	State employment service
90 days	**Reemployment:** Apply to your former employer for reemployment.	Employer

continued

Time Frame	Benefits	Where to Apply
120 days or 1 year beyond with evidence of insurability; or up to 1 year if totally disabled	**VGLI (Veterans' Group Life Insurance):** SGLI may be connected to a five-year term coverage known as VGLI. Coverage may be in amounts of $50,000, $40,000, $30,000, $20,000, or $10,000, but not more than the SGLI amount at the time of separation. At the end of the five-year term, VGLI may be converted to an individual commercial policy with a participating insurance company at standard premium rates regardless of health.	Office of Servicemen's Group Life Insurance 213 Washington Street Newark, NJ 07102 or any VA office
Time varies	**Veterans' Job Training:** Assistance is available for apprenticeship training, on-the-job training, and special job-training programs funded by the government.	State employment service, U.S. Department of Labor, or any VA office
No time limit	**Nonservice-connected Disability or Death Pension:** Veterans with qualifying wartime service who have reached age 65 or who are permanently or totally disabled due to nonservice-connected disabilities may be eligible to receive a monthly pension benefit depending on their income. Surviving spouses and dependent children may also qualify.	Any VA office
Time varies	**Burial plot/interment entitlement:** The VA provides certain benefits to assist with the burial expenses of veterans and certain dependents or survivors. Assistance for burial of dependents and survivors is limited to interment in national cemeteries.	VA national cemetery having grave space or any VA office

continued

Time Frame	Benefits	Where to Apply
No time limit	**Readjustment counseling:** Veterans who served on active duty during the Vietnam era may receive counseling to help in readjusting to civilian life. **Special Note**	Any Veterans' Center, VA hospital, or VA office
1 year from date of the notification of the initial determination	**Appeal to Board of Veterans' Appeals:** Prospective VA beneficiary claimants have the right to appeal determinations made by a VA regional office or medical center. Appellate review will be initiated by a Notice of Disagreement and completed by a substantive appeal after a statement of the case has been furnished.	Department of Veterans Affairs facility responsible for making the determination

Appendix 5

Foreign Opportunities

As a veteran, you are better aware than most Americans about the effects of growing democracy around the world. Calls for help are more frequent from Eastern Europe, East and West Africa, the Pacific Rim, the People's Republic of China, and selected states in the former Soviet Union. You may also have noticed that international investment and lending agencies have dramatically increased their funds for education, training, infrastructure development, and technology transfers. Most countries receiving development funds look to the United States experience for direction and help. They are in a hurry and would rather adopt or adapt a successful method or technology than spend time and money on their own research and development.

There are numerous agencies around the world that would love to have you in their "skilled and available" consultant registry. For those of you who don't want to spend long periods overseas, short-term, well-paid consultant opportunities are available. Full-time (one to three years) consultants are in greatest demand. There are many kinds of agencies looking for you. Register with the following organizations if you are interested:

★ World Bank

★ U.S. Aid for International Development (USAID)

★ Asian Development Bank (ADB)

★ African Development Bank

★ Caribbean Development Bank

★ International Labor Organization (ILO)

★ United Nations Development Program

★ Trade and Development Program—Department of State (TDP)

★ United Nations Industrial Development Organization (UNIDO)

Getting your registration forms submitted and approved with these agencies can be very time consuming. Nonetheless, they could result in exciting, flexible, well-paid opportunities to work around the world! Some believe the international opportunities currently available represent the most challenging, exciting, and financially rewarding experiences for those who like to move around. For detailed information and addresses on any of the organizations listed, contact your congressional office, state office of development, or local library.

VGM CAREER BOOKS

CAREER DIRECTORIES
Careers Encyclopedia
Dictionary of Occupational
  Titles
Occupational Outlook
  Handbook

CAREERS FOR
Animal Lovers
Bookworms
Computer Buffs
Crafty People
Culture Lovers
Environmental Types
Film Buffs
Foreign Language
  Aficionados
Good Samaritans
Gourmets
History Buffs
Kids at Heart
Nature Lovers
Night Owls
Number Crunchers
Shutterbugs
Sports Nuts
Travel Buffs

CAREERS IN
Accounting; Advertising;
Business; Child Care;
Communications;
Computers; Education;
Engineering; Finance;
Government; Health Care;
High Tech; Journalism; Law;
Marketing; Medicine;
Science; Social &
Rehabilitation Services

CAREER PLANNING
Admissions Guide to
  Selective Business Schools
Beginning Entrepreneur
Career Planning &
  Development for College
  Students & Recent
  Graduates
Career Change

Careers Checklists
Cover Letters They Don't
  Forget
Executive Job Search
  Strategies
Guide to Basic Cover Letter
  Writing
Guide to Basic Resume
  Writing
Joyce Lain Kennedy's Career
  book
Out of Uniform
Slam Dunk Resumes
Successful Interviewing for
  College Seniors

CAREER PORTRAITS
Animals
Music
Sports
Teaching

GREAT JOBS FOR
English Majors
Foreign Language Majors
History Majors
Psychology Majors

HOW TO
Approach an Advertising
  Agency and Walk Away
  with the Job You Want
Bounce Back Quickly After
  Losing Your Job
Change Your Career
Choose the Right Career
Find Your New Career Upon
  Retirement
Get & Keep Your First Job
Get Hired Today
Get into the Right Law
  School
Have a Winning Job Interview
Hit the Ground Running in
  Your New Job
Improve Your Study Skills
Jump Start a Stalled Career
Land a Better Job

Launch Your Career in TV
  News
Make the Right Career Moves
Market Your College Degree
Move from College into a
  Secure Job
Negotiate the Raise You
  Deserve
Prepare a *Curriculum Vitae*
Prepare for College
Run Your Own Home
  Business
Succeed in College
Succeed in High School
Write a Winning Resume
Write Successful Cover
  Letters
Write Term Papers & Reports
Write Your College
  Application Essay

OPPORTUNITIES IN
This extensive series provides
detailed information on
nearly 150 individual career
fields.

RESUMES FOR
Advertising Careers
Banking and Financial
  Careers
Business Management
  Careers
College Students &
  Recent Graduates
Communications Careers
Education Careers
Engineering Careers
Environmental Careers
Health and Medical Careers
High School Graduates
High Tech Careers
Midcareer Job Changes
Sales and Marketing Careers
Scientific and Technical
  Careers
Social Service Careers
The First-Time Job Hunter

 VGM Career Horizons
a division of *NTC Publishing Group*
4255 West Touhy Avenue
Lincolnwood, Illinois 60646–1975